Cody

The Extraordinary Life of an Ordinary Dog

Lauren Henry Brehm

Dedicated to Keith Henry, my partner in training and loving all the dogs who came into our lives. Thank you for seeing something special in Cody and helping nurture him to become a Real Dog.

And for all the dogs who live forever in my heart, especially Beowolf, Cody, and Shenanigans.

Chapter 1

Katrina Refugee

Cody with his nose in a corner

WE WERE WATCHING television when Fran turned off the lights.

It was September 5, 1996. We were in Garner, NC—a town outside of Raleigh, the state capital. My husband Keith, our 11-year-old daughter Robyn, and I were concerned about family and friends in the expected path of Hurricane Fran, which was predicted to make land-fall near Cape Fear and Wilmington and turn northeast, following the North Carolina coast. When the lights went out, we assumed the outer bands of the large storm had affected the power grid. We lit some candles, and I continued hemming the shirt I was making. We talked and laughed. One thing we didn't do was worry about ourselves. Raleigh had not sustained a direct hit from a hurricane since Hazel in 1954, so we had no reason to believe Fran would pose any danger to us.

The lights had gone out around 8 p.m. Three hours later, the power was still off. We could hear the wind howling in its unearthly voice, rattling windows and doors like an avenging spirit seeking entry. Evidently, we were closer to the path of the hurricane than originally anticipated. We decided to sleep downstairs in the living room so we would be protected from falling trees or other debris. Even the cats and the dog sheltered with us. It felt like an indoor camping adventure, with sheets on the sofa, sleeping bags on the floor, and flashlights positioned nearby.

I woke up at about 2:00 in the morning to find Keith and Robyn also awake, listening intently. The world outside was eerily silent. The silence was more frightening than the storm had been.

"Why is it so quiet?" asked Robyn, nervously. "Is the hurricane over?"

We admitted we didn't know. "Maybe we're dead, and this is the afterlife," I joked.

"Or maybe everyone else is dead," suggested Keith, "and we're the only ones left." Robyn rolled her eyes at us, an expression familiar to parents of preteen girls. Soon, the wind and rain started up again, roaring their frustration at their inability to enter our home or lure us outside. Keith and I, having been through other hurricanes, realized the silence was the eye of the storm passing overhead. We figured Fran must have turned northwest from Wilmington instead of following the coast. With the sounds of the storm raging around us like a lullaby, we all went back to sleep.

The next morning dawned sunny and clear. We were lucky; the only damage our property had sustained was a broken fence rail where a tree limb had fallen, though the large branch had smashed a play gym on the other side of the fence. We assumed Garner had escaped the worst of it; however, when we went to the shopping center up the street and spoke with other dazed neighbors, we learned the Raleigh area had actually taken a direct hit from Hurricane Fran, the first in over 40 years. The trees that had grown up since Hurricane Hazel had never been tested by gale-force winds, with the result that Fran had leveled over 4,000 trees in Raleigh alone. The storm's flooding had contaminated the local water system, and customers were being warned to boil water before drinking it. The school system was closed, too—even if the power had been on, the streets were impassable due to the downed trees and power lines. We would later learn from news reports that Fran had killed 37 people, 24 of whom were from North Carolina. Damage was estimated to be $5 billion, with almost half of that number coming from North Carolina.

Losing a single fence rail seemed irrelevant in the face of such widespread loss.

At the time, I was recovering from what had politely been referred to as a nervous breakdown. I had been released from a seven-day stay in a psychiatric hospital just five weeks earlier. Upon my release, I wasn't able to do anything on my own. Coping with the stresses that had led to my hospitalization had left me without any judgement or decision-making ability. Medication adjustments left me temporarily unable to drive. I couldn't even go to the grocery store on my own. My recovery was proceeding well, but slowly.

Trying to survive the heat of late summer in North Carolina without refrigeration, water, or air-conditioning was more than I was able to currently handle. We packed a few belongings and headed west, taking the dog, but leaving the cats with an ample supply of food and fresh water. We didn't know how long we would be away, but we knew it wouldn't be longer than the food supply would last. We spent a night and a day as tourists in the Blue Ridge Mountains—normally a pleasant outing, but not under those circumstances. The scenery was as awe-inspiring as ever, but we were too preoccupied with worry and anxiety to enjoy it. On the second evening, our neighbor called and left a message on our home voicemail to let us know that the power was back on. It had only been off 48 hours. We bought enough bottled water to last until the boil order was lifted, went home immediately, and cleaned out several hundred dollars' worth of spoiled food from the refrigerator. Of all the hurricanes I have lived through, Fran was the most personally devastating.

I was able to empathize on a deeply personal level with the destruction I saw on television when Hurricane Katrina hit the Gulf Coast in August, 2005, devastating New Orleans. Katrina caused $81 million in damage and killed over 1,800 people. I was especially worried about the 100,000 pets who had been left behind when their owners evacuated to shelters; 70,000 of those pets perished in the storm. The 30,000 survivors were reunited with their owners or adopted by other families in the weeks following the storm. A few ended up in shelters, waiting for their families to find them or to be adopted into a new home.

In February, 2006, I saw a news report on a cable network saying a temporary shelter that had cared for displaced pets after Katrina was closing. The 70 or so pets that remained homeless were going to be dispersed to shelters throughout the nation when the temporary shelter closed. Unfortunately, the permanent shelter in New Orleans was already filled to capacity and wasn't able to accept any more animals. The newscaster asked professionals in rescue agencies to contact *Best Friends, Inc*—the agency running the temporary shelter—if they were interested in taking any of the remaining dogs. Although I had worked as a volunteer, not as a professional, I contacted *Best Friends*. They put me in touch with Patty, the director of a small animal rescue organization in Sadorus, Illinois, since hers was the rescue nearest to my home in Urbana.

Patty told me about the three dogs she had received from the New Orleans shelter. Two were Chow mixes, while the third was a yellow Labrador retriever. The Chows were adjusting well to being in a new place, but the Lab wasn't. He seemed to get along with the Chows, whom he had known in the temporary shelter, but not the other dogs in the household, and he didn't interact at all with the humans. Patty had tried everything, but nothing seemed to help.

Although I was at that time an English as a Second Language teacher, working part-time at a two-year college, I'd had a lot of experience teaching children with emotional and learning difficulties. The skills that made me effective with children who were withdrawn were the same skills I needed in helping skittish dogs—patience and kindness. My nurturing personality tended to elicit trust from the children. I had seen much the same thing in working with shelter animals; the shy ones usually warmed up to me. I was sure I could help. At the same time, I knew my three dogs, Pepper, Beowolf, and Rascal, were experienced hands at rehabilitating foster dogs. Keith was a supportive partner in caring for needy animals, so I wouldn't be taking on the challenge alone; I had lost count of the number of dogs we had fostered in our home to rehabilitate and train when we lived in Tallahassee. My decision was an easy one, and I agreed to foster Cody, the withdrawn Lab.

Cody entered the house at a crouch, his belly dragging against the floor. Patty held one end of his leash, but Cody was glued to her side even when she let it go. He didn't react to me when I tried to greet him, so I ignored him for the moment. When Patty stepped outside to get something from her car, Cody scuttled into a corner near my desk and stayed there, his nose buried in the space between the desk and the wall. He seemed to believe if he couldn't see me, I couldn't see him.

I'd kept my three dogs outside for the moment so they wouldn't overwhelm Cody. I brought Beowolf in first, since he was both the pack leader and the gentlest of the dogs. Beo was curious about the new dog, but he didn't have much time to get to know him. I must not have latched the back door securely, because Pepper and Rascal came running in a minute later and interrupted the getting acquainted process. Fortunately, they all sensed Cody's fear, and everyone behaved appropriately, with no growling or barking.

After Patty left, I read over the information *Best Friends* had compiled. Cody was probably under 2 years old. He had been found on the streets of New Orleans in November, 2005, about 3 months after the storm, dirty and malnourished, with a chain collar embedded in his neck.

Dogs are naturally clean animals and won't soil their sleeping and eating areas if they have a choice, but while Cody was at the shelter, he had been too afraid to walk across a floor to go outside to eliminate, so he would do it wherever he was. One of the *Best Friends* volunteers had taken special care of Cody, carrying him outside for potty breaks. He had spent most of his day at her feet, hiding his head under her desk. When she walked away, Cody would follow in a crouch. Now that he had left that safe setting, he had reverted to his previous behavior.

Skittish hardly seemed like an adequate word to describe how truly terrified this dog was. He was trying to make himself invisible. His body was curled into as tight a ball as he could form. His head was turned away; I couldn't even see his eyes. Cody shivered at every new noise, the flesh on his back rippling like a pond disturbed by a pebble. He didn't know what to expect in this new setting, and his uncertainty expressed itself as fear.

One of the more intriguing things I found in Cody's file was a notation that indicated the name "Rex" and the date of his last rabies vaccine, which was before the hurricane. Cody wore a rabies tag on the faded red and green striped collar he was wearing. I thought it was possible *Best Friends* had been able to trace the tag back to the vet clinic that had vaccinated Cody, and from there had been able to learn his original name, his owner's name, and the date he had received his rabies vaccine. I didn't know if that meant Rex/Cody's original owner had perished in the storm, if he didn't want Cody back, or if *Best Friends* had decided not to allow the owner to take Cody back, considering his embedded collar was a sign of serious neglect.

Cody's owner must have placed the chain collar around Cody's neck when he was much younger and smaller and never checked it again. As Cody grew, the collar became tighter around his neck, eventually growing into his flesh. I'd seen something similar happen to trees, when someone tied a rope or chain around a trunk and left it there as the tree grew around it. Cody's collar had to be surgically removed. The surgery, along with his neutering, took place on New Year's Eve, 2005.

Poor guy! What a way to ring in a New Year!

If Cody was two years old when I met him in March, 2006, then I calculated he was born in New Orleans in Spring, 2004. Although nothing concrete is known about his life before he was rescued in the aftermath of Hurricane Katrina, I can make educated guesses about what his early life was like based on how he reacted to things later on. He hated confinement. He was wary around men. He flinched when anyone raised a hand, even if it was just to gesture or to pet him. He accepted women easily, but it took him months to warm up to men enough to let them touch him. He hated loud noises, even applause. He was especially terrified by thunder and fireworks. The condition Cody was found in suggests he was the victim of a certain mindset on how dogs should be treated.

Based on the available evidence, I think Cody's first two

years of life went something like this: he was a quiet, shy puppy, possibly the runt of his litter. Though just as intelligent as his litter mates, he was more submissive than they were. As his brothers and sisters wrestled with him, Cody was always the first to roll onto his back, displaying his vulnerable belly in a show of submission. However, Cody was undisturbed by being a low-ranking member of his litter; he preferred to be alone, watching the world and learning from what he saw.

Cody watched as one by one his litter mates left with people who would give them a loving, forever home. Cody, the shy, loner pup, didn't approach these strangers as they came to *ooh!* and *aah!* over the puppies and choose one special dog to take home. Cody didn't jump up on the people, didn't lick their hands, and didn't scamper. Cody watched from a distance. Thus, Cody was never chosen.

Eventually, someone took Cody from his mother's owner. Cody's new owner knew a yellow Lab would be a good watch dog, and he knew just how to turn any dog into a watch dog, no matter how gentle the dog might start out being. Everyone knows that if you want to make a dog mean, you treat him mean. Chain him up outside. Don't let him in the house, or you'll turn him into a sissy dog. You want him to guard your property, not your bedroom. Yell at him. Beat him. Treat him like you want him to treat the strangers that come onto your property: mean.

There are several problems with what "everyone knows." The first is that the guarding instinct in dogs is based on the instinct to protect the pack's territory. If you want your dog to protect your property, you first have to make him part of your pack. If you live in the house, so should he. He should eat and sleep where the rest of the pack is, meaning the human family and any other pets in the household—that way he'll do everything he can to protect the members of his pack and the territory they occupy.

The second problem is that when a dog lives only outside, he thinks all of the outside is his to protect. Instead of a dog who protects your property and only your property, you end up with a dog who tries to protect everything from everyone. He barks at every passerby and every sound that disturbs the silence. If you live in a busy area, especially with lots of kids around, your dog will bark all the time, annoying you and your neighbors. A dog that barks all the time can't be relied on to give a warning when danger threatens your home.

Finally, the process of turning a dog "mean" is highly fallible. If you yell at and beat a dog to make him mean, what you teach him is fear and distrust. He believes everyone approaching him is going to hurt him. If the dog is somewhat dominant, he may become aggressive, believing he must attack in order to protect himself. You have turned him "mean," but he will attack indiscriminately, including you, your children, and your neighbors.

If, on the other hand, the dog is naturally submissive, he will withdraw further and become more docile, hoping something he does will please you so you will stop beating and yelling at him. All he wants to do is whatever you want him to do, but he can't figure out what that is. Dogs want and need to be told what to do, but yelling and beating only tell them what not to do.

Cody was temperamentally unsuited to be a watchdog. With a gentle trainer with an understanding of doggy psychology, he would eventually have become a member of his family/pack, and been protective of them, but he would never have been willing to attack on command. Under the conditions Cody found himself in, he became nervous and ever more skittish. He developed fears of everything. Living outside, and especially in hot, humid Louisiana, he learned that thunder accompanied lightning and rain, all things he disliked. All loud noises reminded him of both yelling and thunder. Being fearful resulted in more scoldings and beatings, resulting in even more fear.

Cody was probably terrified out of his mind when Hurricane Katrina hit, with hours upon hours of rain, wind, lightning, and thunder. Whether his owner released him during the storm to save himself or he broke free on his own, Cody became a stray. He wandered the streets of New Orleans, trying to find food. He didn't want to challenge other dogs for the scraps he could find, but he also didn't want to starve. He got into at least one fight that left him with a scar on his muzzle. Someone shot at him, leaving a piece of shrapnel in one ear. He stayed away from humans after that, and became so good at avoiding people, it took three months before someone was able to catch him.

Chapter 2

All the Dogs I've Loved Before

L to R: Rascal, Beowolf, Pepper

I WAS BORN on Christmas Day, 1958, on Long Island in New York. My parents grew up in Brooklyn and met in college, marrying after my father returned from a free, all-expense paid trip with the Army after his graduation. They divorced when I was three years old; my mother moved to Queens along with her dog Napoleon, my younger brother Mark, and me.

Napoleon, my mother's grey toy poodle, had been a fixture in my life since I was a few months old; the dog was older than I was by a month. When we were four years old, Nappy got hit by a car. My grandfather came to babysit while my mother and grandmother took the injured dog to the vet. Grandpa was trying to explain to me that Nappy was going to lose his foot. Although I was a precocious child, I didn't understand what Grandpa was saying; I had no frame of reference for understanding a lost limb. Grandpa picked up the dog's brush, a palm-sized wooden brush with a leather handle, and tried to demonstrate how a prosthetic foot might be attached; this just confused me, especially when Nappy returned home without a wooden brush at the end of his leg. After a while, it seemed normal that Nappy had four legs and three feet. He got around as well as any other dog, and remained devoted to my mother for his entire 15-year life.

When Nappy and I were nine, my mother decided Mark and I needed a dog of our own, though I hasten to add we had not asked for one. My mother wanted another dog, and decided we presented a viable reason for getting one. In Spring 1968, she bought a beagle puppy, whom we named Ottavio after a character in one of my mother's community theater plays.

Mother told Mark and me we were responsible for taking care of Ottavio, but since we hadn't wanted him in the first place, we weren't willing to accept responsibility for him; we were barely willing to help when asked. We didn't see him as "our" dog. Our mother told us she was going to house-train the puppy, and put down newspaper on all the floors, everywhere Ottavio could reach. Her reasoning seemed to be that anywhere the puppy peed or pooped would be on the paper; therefore, he would be paper-trained. However, she never picked up what Ottavio deposited on the papers, nor did she ever change the papers unless we expected company. Our apartment was carpeted in dried out newspapers, yellowed with urine rather than age, with little piles of dog poop of various vintages, from fresh to white-crusted, dotting the paper like so many random punctuation marks. My grandmother was often critical about our apartment's condition. I became self-conscious about the poop and avoided having friends in the house.

When I was ten, my mother earned her master's degree in early childhood education. The teacher of the laboratory kindergarten program at East Carolina University had just retired. The state didn't offer public kindergarten in 1969, so there were few experienced kindergarten teachers in North Carolina at that time; my mother had the experience and knowledge that ECU needed. Relocating gave her a chance to start over away from the influence and interference of her family. Both my grandmother and my aunt frequently complained about my mother's poor housekeeping and overall poor hygiene, both her own and us as her children. We moved in August, 1969, to Greenville, a small college town in eastern North Carolina.

The household situation improved a little when we moved to Greenville. Living in a house rather than an apartment meant the dogs could go outside to potty. Dogs were allowed to run free in Greenville from dawn to dusk, so Ottavio was out of the house most of the time. Unfortunately, Mother added cats to the household, and didn't take care of the cats any better than she had taken care of the dogs. If the litter box was full, the cats did their business wherever they wanted, inside or out. If it was raining outside, the dogs would lift their legs against the furniture. Our house stank.

When a child grows up in a certain environment, they tend to assume everyone else does the same things their own family does. It's only when they start spending significant time in their friends' homes or live on their own that they see differences. While I had had friends in New York, I hadn't spent much time in their homes, and none of them had had dogs. Most of the friends I made in junior high and high school also hadn't had dogs. I couldn't imagine other people's dogs were any better trained than my mother's dogs because that was all I'd ever been exposed to.

When I married Keith in 1979 and left my mother's home, I

was determined I would never have dogs. There was no way I would ever live the way my mother did. Cats were easier: provide a food dish, water dish, and a litter box, and you were done. They wouldn't make a mess unless the humans neglected to keep the litter box clean. Most of the cats I had known were friendly and affectionate, much as a dog would be. Keith and I got our first kitten, Ariel, about a month after we married.

Five years later, when our daughter Robyn was born, our cat Princess used to let us know when the baby was crying by trotting down the stairs to the bottom step and letting out a howl. If we didn't respond, the cat would seek us out and howl again. We were never sure if Princess did that because she was worried about Robyn's welfare or because the crying hurt her ears and she wanted us to make it stop; either way, she was good at being a protector, just like a dog would have been.

Still, I had grown up reading books in which the heroes of the story were dogs: *Big Red, Lassie Come Home,* and *The Heart of a Dog.* There was something special about living with a dog, and the bond between human and dog was unique. A dog could be a friend in a way a cat wasn't. Although I was the one saying "no dogs allowed", I missed having one around.

My opinion of dogs changed at Thanksgiving, 1995, when my student's family invited my family to share their holiday meal. The family lived with Tasha and Tucker, two beautiful and beautifully behaved black Labrador retrievers. The house was immaculate, without a single yellow newspaper in sight; Tasha and Tucker obviously didn't soil inside. The dogs were happy, and they were an integral part of the family. They didn't jump up on people or furniture. They didn't beg for food from either family or guests. Both of them gave and accepted affection within their family and approached us, as strangers, with friendly curiosity.

After dinner, I complimented Mrs. S. on the dogs' behavior.

"How did you get them so well-behaved? Did you take them to an obedience class? Hire a trainer?"

"Nah, we just trained them ourselves," she answered.

"But how did you know what to do?" I persisted.

"Well, it's just like parenting. Read through the books until you find one you agree with. Then follow that one."

Books? I was stunned. You mean they write books about how to train dogs?

Despite being a bibliophile with a houseful of books and a well-worn library card, I'd never even thought about that possibility. Over the next month, I read nearly everything the local library had on dog training, from the Monks of New Skete to Karen Pryor to Carol Lea Benjamin, whose book, *Mother Knows Best: The Natural Way to Train Your Dog*, ended up being my favorite. Benjamin's philosophy was built on observations of how mother dogs disciplined their pups. The puppies were born wired to learn and understand canine communication. We could continue training by using similar methods, adapted for use by humans. I realized my background in special education would blend perfectly with training a dog. I had taught numerous parents about using logical and natural consequences in managing their children's behavior. Now I was simply going to apply the same principles in raising a puppy. After a month of nonstop reading, I got my first dog.

Bentley came to live with us when he was 9 weeks old, and I took him to the vet for a check-up the next day. I was proud that I impressed the vet with how well-prepared I was for dog ownership; I was able to answer every question the vet asked. *Why was I adding a dog to the family?* Because I wanted a friend and companion. *Why had I chosen a Lab?* I had been looking for dog breeds that were smart, friendly, family dogs. My short list included German shepherds, collies, and Labradors. *How was I going to house train him?* I thought crate-training was a good method. The dog spends time in his crate except when he can be supervised. As he learns to go outside to potty, he gets to spend longer periods of time out of his crate. Then the vet stumped me; he asked me why I named the puppy Bentley. I told him that after hours of poring through puppy name books, I liked that name best. The vet was disappointed there wasn't some fanciful or logical story behind the name. He advised me to come up with a better story for Bentley's name. Unfortunately, I never did.

Having a puppy is a lot like having a newborn baby in the house. Bentley would awaken us at 3:00 in the morning with pitiful crying, asking to be taken outside. I learned to be grateful that dog bladders develop control sooner than human bladders; two years of 3 a.m. walks would have killed me.

We spent many hours sitting in the family room watching Bentley pounce on his toys with a growl and a little death shake. Keith and I had spent hours watching in the same way when the cute baby in the room had been Robyn, 11 years earlier. In fact, Robyn started to become jealous of the attention we were giving to Bentley. She was an only child who was finally learning what the phrase "sibling rivalry" meant.

Bentley was a black Lab, just like the ones at my student's home, but that was coincidence. His mom was from breeding stock, but his dad was the Lab from down the street who had jumped the fence. Bentley was the most handsome Lab I had ever seen, and possibly the most intelligent. He understood human conversations better than he should have.

One afternoon a handyman was at our house, working on the fence. That day he'd brought his young son with him. When the boy left part of his lunch—a single pickle—sitting on a step, his dad cautioned him that the dog might take it. Bentley listened to the conversation, walked over to the unattended pickle, and scarfed it down. He hadn't so much as noticed it until the handyman had mentioned it.

The best thing about Bentley was learning how happy living with a dog made me. I never felt lonely with Bentley beside me. He was nine months old when I had my nervous breakdown, which led to my being disabled; Bentley was always with me, my constant companion. While I was unable to work, Keith asked the educational software company he worked with for a position in sales rather than training; the raise he would get, plus potential commissions, would compensate for the loss of my income. They hired him for a territory in the Florida panhandle, and we moved to Tallahassee just after Bentley's first birthday. We left about 5:00 at night, after the movers had emptied our house, and drove through the night with three humans, two cats, and one dog in a Camry. The sedative didn't work on one of the cats, and she yowled during the whole drive; it wasn't the kind of road trip they make buddy movies about.

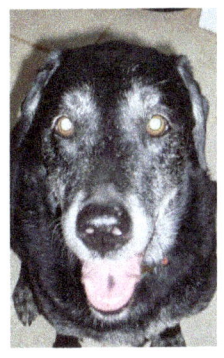

Pepper in her older years

When Bentley was about 18 months old, his vet asked me if I would be interested in adopting another dog. An 8-month-old female black Lab had been rescued from downtown Tallahassee, near the university, and she needed a home. The man who had rescued her from the street had taken her home, but she hadn't been able to get along with his German shepherd. He was willing to pay all her rescue bills, including spaying, but he couldn't offer her a permanent home. I adopted her. She was easier to name than Bentley had been. Her color and her spicy temperament made Pepper the perfect name.

Bentley and Pepper were typical siblings. They played together and napped together. Sometimes the playing got rough and someone got hurt. They fought over toys; each dog's favorite was the toy the other one had. They wouldn't share. Pepper cried whenever Bentley took her teddy bear. I had to buy a second dog crate for Pepper because Bentley wouldn't let her use his even for a minute.

Bentley especially wouldn't share me. When I was petting Pepper, Bentley nosed between us for his share. If Bentley was on the bed to take a nap with me, and Pepper tried to get up, Bentley growled at her, but if Pepper got on the bed first, Bentley went to his crate and sulked. When I tried to work with Pepper on basic obedience commands, Bentley stood nearby and performed all his tricks, trying to get a cookie, too. Mostly, though, they loved each other and hated being separated for any reason.

Pepper was a wild woman. She was hyperactive and did everything at top speed. When I gave her a bowl of water on her first night with me, she splashed in it with both her front paws, spraying water all over the kitchen. She would jump into any body of water of any size, from puddle to ocean, but she hated to be out in the rain. When she would escape from our house, as happened from time to time, she took off in a straight line. Keith would run after her while I got Bentley and the leashes into the car and tried to head Pepper off, using Bentley as the bait. We always caught her when she ran out of steam and wanted a ride home.

Pepper loved hunting lizards, which were abundant in Florida. She would swallow them whole, then throw them up. One time she rushed a window to get at a lizard on the outside. Instead of catching the lizard, she broke one of the two panes of glass, cut her nose and the pad of her paw, and got blood all over Keith's home office. Keith and I rushed Pepper to the vet, leaving Robyn to walk into the house after school to find no parents, no note, a broken window, and blood everywhere. The injuries didn't slow Pepper down a bit, but during her recovery, she learned she liked to be petted and cared for as opposed to her former habit of not holding still long enough for petting. She became an affection sponge.

One of Pepper's favorite things to do was to put her front paws on the shoulders of someone sitting on the sofa. She would slide her back paws onto their lap so she was sitting on them; Pepper apparently thought she was a "Laprador" retriever. Once she was situated, Pepper would lick the person's ear. If the person turned their head to get her to stop, she would lick the other ear. We had no clue why she did that. She was prone to ear infections, so perhaps she was trying to take care of our ears the way we took care of hers.

One time we took both dogs to the beach. Bentley loved to body surf. He would swim out into the ocean and catch waves back in. Since Pepper was still a flight risk at the time, she had to stay on her leash. I took her out to a depth of about waist to chest high on me, and let her paddle around. Bentley swam over to me and tried to get Pepper to ride a wave with him. He showed her how to do it, and came back to where I was. I told Bentley that Pepper had to stay on her leash, and he tried to take Pepper's leash from my hand, as if to say *don't worry, I'll watch out for her.* Nice try, Bentley!

Around the same time I adopted Pepper, I began volunteering for the Tallahassee Leon Community Animal Service Center. My job description was to help customers find the dog they wanted to adopt. I noticed some of the dogs didn't have the interactive skills necessary to sell themselves: they didn't approach the door of their kennels, make eye contact with the customers, or act "cute." The kill rate at the shelter was 60%-70% at the time, so learning those skills was potentially life-saving for those dogs. With that in mind, I started doing what I called "dog therapy."

Whenever I didn't have customers to assist, I would enter a dog's kennel and interact with them. The kennels were fairly large, with a guillotine door separating the inside and outside sections; I lowered the guillotine so the dogs couldn't go outside and get away from me. Some dogs were thrilled to have me pet and cuddle them. With those dogs, I gave them little treats, and left the kennel. I would stop by a few more times during a 2-3 hour shift, and greet them, pet them, and give them treats through the chain link door. That was all they needed to learn to approach the door when people came to look at them. A lot of my dogs got adopted, and I firmly believe it was because they learned how to be cute.

Some dogs didn't understand why they were there or where their family was, and as a result, they became depressed. One day, I watched a man drop off a beautiful yellow Lab, complete with AKC papers and an obedience school diploma. The man was in tears. He and his wife had just had a baby, and she insisted the dog had to go. The man knew what she was asking of him was wrong, but how could he reason with someone who was being unreasonable? The dog cried after his dad left, not understanding why he was in this place and locked up. I comforted the dog as best I could; the danger for him was that he might not be able to overcome his depression enough to attract a new family before his time at the shelter ran out. Fortunately, he was a handsome dog, and all those papers were impressive—he found another home within a few days.

Fearful and/or withdrawn dogs were the hardest for me to work with. They would sit in the back corner of the kennel, facing away from the door, sometimes cowering. When I entered their kennels, they would barely acknowledge my presence. Sometimes their muscles would get a little tense, or they would try to make themselves smaller. I sat as far from them as I could, mindful of my own safety as much as their comfort. I would talk to them softly and gently. Sometimes I would sing to them, usually lullabies I had sung to my daughter. I would often toss a treat close to them. The shelter only had dry dog biscuits, so I started bringing meat snacks from home. With most of the dogs, that was enough to get them interested and gave me a reasonable starting point for working with them.

Then there were the hard-core cases, dogs that were so overwhelmed they weren't able to respond. I struggled to find a way to reach them without frightening them or endangering myself. I started to offer those dogs my shoe to smell. I don't know why I thought of it. I think I was imitating what some pediatricians do with toddlers, which is to examine their shoes first. For toddlers, their shoes are an extension of themselves, so if the doctor puts her stethoscope on the shoe, the toddler is more likely to accept it on his body. I think I also figured feet are stinky, and dogs love stinky things. They learn from smells, so why not offer the dogs a chance to get to know me without interacting directly?

For whatever reason, my shoe trick worked. Dogs that had previously been shaking in a corner suddenly turned around to sniff my shoe. I wasn't always able to pet them, but I could usually get them to take a treat from me, and I could often make eye contact with them. As with the less traumatized dogs, once I left their kennel, I would come back, stand at the door, and call to them softly, holding out a treat. Once they trusted me, they were able to approach the door. Some of them generalized that behavior to other people at their kennel doors, and thus were able to be adopted.

While I was a volunteer at the shelter, animal control officers in Bay County, Florida, found dozens of dogs who had been abused and neglected by their owner, a supposed breeder of hunting dogs. Corpses of dead dogs littered the property. Some dogs in kennels and cages had sores on their legs from standing knee-high in their own filth. All the dogs were emaciated. Some were too sick to rescue and were put down immediately. The local shelter couldn't take all of the rest, so the dogs were sent throughout the state to other shelters. All the shelters that took the dogs had to promise not to euthanize them. Our shelter received about 10 of them.

Some of the dogs were friendly, and didn't need my help at all; they simply needed to put on weight and find good homes. Some were skittish, but responded well to my overtures of friendship. There was one dog, a black and tan coonhound, that needed everything I could give him. I could count every bone in his body through his dull, dusty coat. His tail was permanently tucked between his legs. Every time I entered his kennel, he peed submissively, usually on me, and averted his head and eyes. I worked with him every day while he was in the shelter. I was more forceful with him than I usually was, putting my hand lightly on his flank without waiting for him to acknowledge my presence. I knew he would never accept me until he knew I was harmless. I had to show him I was harmless by doing something outside his comfort zone, but he would like. Closeness and petting were my best tools, along with tempting treats.

I can't say I had a lot of success with my coonhound, but I had some. He stopped peeing on me, which I considered a win. He wouldn't look at me, but he no longer automatically got to his feet and moved away when I entered his kennel. Lying down next to him, and petting him in long, gentle strokes from shoulder to flank, I could feel his muscles relax, just a little.

I didn't have a lot of time with him, just a little over a week. His photo had been on the front page of our local newspaper with a story about the dogs the shelter had received. One worker at the paper was so moved by the story that she and her husband came to the shelter specifically to adopt my baby. I got to talk with both of them, and tell them what I was doing with him. I'm glad his story had a happy ending, finding a forever home with two people who were willing to give him the time, patience, and love he needed to live a long and happy life. Until I met Cody, that coonhound was the neediest dog I had ever worked with.

In contrast to my coonhound, Bentley's story didn't have a happy ending. By the time Bentley was four months old, he was showing signs of aggression, initially over food. Being a first-time dog owner, I didn't recognize the problem at the time. There were seemingly minor incidents where he growled at Robyn as if she were another dog rather than one of the humans in charge. At other times he had growled at people, including those in the house, possibly to protect me—or so I had thought—but probably to keep others from taking my attention from him. I took him to an obedience class, and he did well. In fact, the first time he attacked me, just after his second birthday, he stopped when I gave him the command to go into his crate.

His attack came the morning after we returned from a short trip. Bentley had missed me, but instead of being clingy and demanding my attention, he seemed angry at me for having been gone. When I tried to end our morning cuddle and get out of bed, he attacked. Over the next three months, I worked with his vet, a private trainer, and consultants from the School of Veterinary Medicine at Tufts University to try to get his behavior under control. We tried anxiety medication, changes in routine, more obedience training, and eventually an anti-depressant, but nothing helped.

The second time Bentley attacked me, I was sitting on the

sofa, crocheting. I don't remember what the trigger was, but Bentley lunged at me. I threw the afghan I was making over his head, and thereby avoided being bitten. We got the basket-style muzzle the trainer had suggested and placed it over his face. Bentley was furious and kept barking and lunging. Bentley's vet was out of town, so I called the trainer to ask her what to do next. She could hear Bentley's barks over the phone and told me the only other time she'd heard a dog make those sounds was when she watched *Old Yeller*, and that dog had been rabid. It was obvious Bentley was too aggressive to live with humans. It was a Saturday evening; I took him to the vet to be put down on Monday. I stayed with him as the drug took effect, petting him and telling him I was sorry his life had turned out this way. He was just a little over two years old.

Losing Bentley was incredibly difficult, but it was also a relief. None of us in the household, human or animal, had realized how much Bentley had been holding us hostage to his aggressive behavior. The first evening without Bentley, Pepper walked into his crate instead of her own at dinner time. I told her to get into her own crate, which she did. At bedtime that night, Pepper lay down on the floor on my side of the bed, which had always been Bentley's place. I woke up the next morning to find Pepper lying across the foot of the bed in her usual place. She never again slept in Bentley's old place. I think she was telling me she knew he was gone, and maybe that she was glad.

Bentley's death left an aching dog-shaped hole in my heart. I kept breaking into tears every time my thoughts wandered to Bentley, no matter where I was. Conventional wisdom suggests waiting until you're no longer mourning for your dog before getting another. I don't pay much attention to conventional wisdom. At the end of a week, I decided nothing other than another dog could fill that hole in my heart and stop the pain that was hemorrhaging from my eyes. Pepper was a great family dog, but she didn't have the bond with me Bentley had had. I missed that bond as much as I missed Bentley himself.

While I worked at the shelter, I kept a lookout for my next dog. I knew I wanted a dog that was friendly and easy-going, even if not super intelligent. I was pretty sure it would be a male, probably from a large breed, and already an adult. I was afraid of adopting another puppy and finding out when that puppy became aggressive that my poor abilities as a dog trainer had caused Bentley's problems rather than something inherent in him. I thought if I could find an adult dog to adopt, I would know exactly what I was getting. I found a temperament test for dogs and kept the directions and a few materials in my smock pocket, so I could test any likely candidates. I tried a couple of dogs, but none of them felt right.

Meanwhile, Linda, one of the animal control officers, asked me to help her vaccinate a litter of pups that had come in. Even though the kennel had had a sign on it saying not to place animals in there for 72 hours because of parvo exposure, someone had put the puppies in there. Parvovirus is a life-threatening infection that usually affects the gastrointestinal tract of young dogs. As a precaution, Linda was giving them the parvo vaccine. She wanted me to hold the pups while she administered the shots.

There were four reddish-brown puppies, three females and one male. The females were all smooth-coated while the male was fluffy and at least half again as big as his sisters. The girls were a typical group of puppies, crawling all over each other, fighting and tussling, while the boy tolerated the abuses his sisters heaped on him without ever joining in. One of the girls left me with a scar on my arm when she scratched me with her back paw while wiggling to avoid the vaccine. The little boy just snuggled while I held him, and didn't react to the shot at all.

I didn't want a puppy, but there was something about that

little guy that spoke to me, so I tested him. His responses were completely atypical. For example, when I threw something that landed away from him, I expected he would either investigate it or be afraid of it. Instead, he followed it with his eyes and lay down. He wasn't disturbed by the noise, but he also didn't care enough to go check it out. Puppy or no, this was the laid-back dog I was looking for.

This was my Beowolf.

Beowolf in his tux

Beowolf grew to be about 85 pounds, with a lanky build. His fur was soft, especially around his shoulders and head, and smelled naturally sweet; people often asked me what kind of perfume or shampoo I used on him, but the truth was that I didn't use anything. Beo had a ferocious bark, with a deep, resonant voice like a German shepherd. He also had a tail that resembled a shepherd's, which he wagged in circles. The rest of him looked like a Rhodesian Ridgeback, but without a ridge. In the summer months, a line of lighter fur ran down his back where the ridge would have been. When people asked me what breed he was, I always said he was a purebred brown dog. If pressed, I would say he was a Rhodesian Ridgeless-back.

Beowolf showed early on that he loved young children. When he was around 5 months old, we had guests over, including an active 2-year-old girl. Sitting down, Beo was taller than the little girl. She was all over the poor dog, hugging him, stepping on him, pulling his ears and tail, and generally tormenting him. He loved it. At one point, he licked her face. She turned right around and licked his face back. When she tried to jump on him, however, he growled. I scolded him and made him get off the sofa they were playing on. That was the only time in his entire life Beowolf ever growled at a human.

Anytime Beowolf saw babies or toddlers being held by someone, he would sit at a distance and whine until he got permission to approach. Then he would sniff their feet. If the children and the parents were agreeable, the kids would sit or stand on the ground, and Beo would get to see them. He would sit straight and tall while the children greeted him. He loved being hugged by little ones; his soft, sweet-smelling fur made hugging him like embracing a living plush toy. Amazingly, given his size, children were rarely afraid of him. It seemed they sensed that he was gentle.

Beowolf and Zeke, a guinea pig

Beowolf also loved small animals, including cats, guinea pigs, and moles. He played with a huge palmetto bug one evening. A palmetto bug, for those not from the Deep South, looks like a large, flying roach. I'm not sure how he caught it, but Beo brought it in from outside and lay down in the living room, keeping the bug between his paws and nudging it with his nose. Pepper was almost frantic; she wanted to eat that bug so badly, but Beo protected his bug from Pepper. He never harmed it, even as he played with it, though his attentions made the bug's wings too wet to fly away. Eventually, I had to take the bug from Beo and let it go—I didn't need another pet.

Another time, Beowolf was nosing around in the grass, his attention evidently caught by something. I went out to see what it was—a mole. I couldn't tell if Beowolf had dug up the poor thing or if he had caught it when it surfaced. Its fur was wet from Beowolf kisses. As I watched, the mole tried to get away. Whichever way it turned, Beowolf would use his snout or his paws to prevent it from going back underground. Eventually, I took pity on the little critter; I took it away from Beowolf and placed it on a wooded traffic island outside our house.

When Beo first came to live with us, we had a dog named Magick, a black and white spaniel-border collie mix. I had seen her at the shelter and couldn't stand the thought of this sweet, friendly little dog being euthanized because she didn't have a home. She had come to live with us as the third member of our pack with Bentley and Pepper, but she never developed a close bond with any of us. I believed from watching her that she wanted to have a special human to bond with just as I had wanted exactly the right dog. In contrast, Pepper didn't seem interested in having her own special human; she was bonded with her family as a whole. After we started fostering, I changed Magick's status to "foster dog," and started looking for a perma-nent home for her. Magick left for her forever home after a few weeks and bonded quickly with her new humans and their ferret.

Magick had been our pack leader at the time. Because of her herding instinct, she nipped the dogs' heels to control their behavior. When Magick left our home, Beowolf became the pack leader and adopted heel-nipping as his discipline method. Cody was the last member of the pack to continue to use heel-nips.

Beowolf was the undisputed leader of our pack, but he was completely submissive to the humans. He obeyed me, but he also adored me. He wanted to be with me wherever I was. If I was going out, he wanted to come along. Unfortunately, he usually got carsick, so I learned not to feed him if I planned to take him out. When we rode together, Beo would stand on the back seat. He was too afraid of the car to relax and lie down. The result was that every time I applied the brakes, Beowolf would fall off the seat, which gave him more reason to be afraid and made him even less likely to relax.

Except for the car, Beo loved being with me. If he could have offered an opinion, I think he would have said he preferred to be with me in the car rather than to be without me at home. The bond I had with Beowolf was built on love and trust, whereas the bond Cody had built with his previous owner had been based on fear. Somehow, I had to teach Cody to trust me. The most effective teacher in that endeavor was Beowolf, who became Cody's role model and mentor.

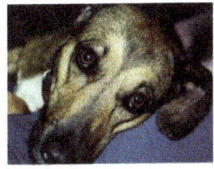

Rascal

Besides Pepper and Beowolf, the other member of the pack when Cody came to live with us was Rascal. He was originally a foster dog and came already named; it would turn out to be the perfect name. Rascal was a handsome dog. He was a hound mix, with a dachshund head perched on a small, muscular beagle body. Rascal's fur had little swirls that looked like rosettes in the white fur on his chest and the brown fur of his bottom. Although short at the shoulder, Rascal weighed 45 pounds. He was built like the proverbial brick privy. When he bumped into someone's leg, he left a bruise.

Rascal had an adorable face. Keith and I thought he looked like Max, the Grinch's dog from the 1966 animated version of *How the Grinch Stole Christmas*. I think the resemblance was in Rascal's eyes. Chuck Jones was the animation genius who brought Dr. Seuss's *Grinch* to life, and his animation style often included eyes that reflected love; Rascal's eyes always looked like a Chuck Jones cartoon. When we were in public together, strangers approached Rascal saying, "Look! It's Max!"

Rascal refused to learn basic commands, though to be honest I didn't push him too hard. When I was handing out treats to the other dogs as rewards for their following obedience commands, all Rascal would do was sit. I finally taught him "Rascal, look cute," at which point he would look at me and wag his tail, looking as cute as a hound dog could possibly look. He always got his treats.

Rascal was a toy chewer. No toy we bought for any of the dogs was allowed to squeak. If the toy had a squeaker, Rascal would perform a 'squeakerectomy' on it at the first chance he got. On at least one occasion his squeakerectomy was delayed by a couple of years, but he eventually got the job done.

Keith and I were sitting side by side on the piano bench one day. Keith picked up Pepper's toy, a ring made of tennis ball material. It still had a squeaker, as we learned when Keith squeaked it, and Pepper came running in to play.

"How does it still have a squeaker?" I wondered. "Why hasn't Rascal desqueakered it yet?"

"Don't know," answered Keith. "Where is the squeaker, anyway?" He turned it over in his hands, ignoring Pepper's attempts to play with it. We peered at it together, searching for the squeaker.

"Well, no wonder it still has a squeaker. If we can't find it, I guess Rascal can't either," I mused.

"Here it is!" exclaimed Keith, pointing to a small opening on the inner edge of the ring.

He squeaked it a few times and tossed it to Pepper, who ran off to play with her prize. Then we noticed Rascal standing half hidden in the doorway. My eyes narrowed with suspicion. "Did he just watch us locate the squeaker for him?"

Later that day, Rascal performed surgery on Pepper's ring; it never squeaked again.

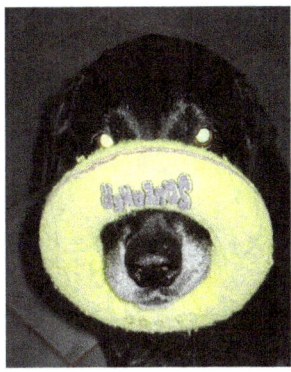

Pepper and her squeakerless ring

Rascal was about a year old when he first arrived at the house. He was perfectly house trained, though that was probably from his own instinct for cleanliness rather than formal training. When I had first taken him to a get-acquainted area at the shelter, he had gone to the fence and peed. And peed. And peed. He had apparently waited until he was out of his kennel before relieving himself. He did the same thing every time I picked him up from the vet's office during his lengthy treatment for worms. As soon as we left the building, he took care of business. The river of pee he created overflowed from the bushes, across the sidewalk, and down the sloping parking lot—and he was still going. I swore that dog would rather explode than pee in the house.

Rascal's other toilet habits were not as tidy. When he got excited and barked, a small piece of poop would often fly out of his butt. We referred to this as Rascal's "reserve turd." We theorized that when he pooped, he always held one back. That way, he could punctuate his warnings to stray dogs and lurking strangers in a particularly concrete way. It was an annoying, but relatively harmless habit. It did tend to limit his world, though. When Keith and I renewed our wedding vows for our 25th anniversary, Beowolf was the ring bearer, and Pepper was the flower dog, but Rascal had to remain at home; we didn't know what might fly out of his butt if he got excited and started barking during the ceremony or at the party afterward.

Rascal came to us riddled with worms: tapeworms, hookworms, and heartworms. He would have to be neutered before he could be adopted, but the rescue group insisted he be wormfree before they would invest in his neutering. The reasoning was that heartworm treatment was difficult for dogs, and some died in the process. With a limited budget available, there was no point in neutering a dog who might die before adoption.

I had been warned that hookworms were notoriously difficult to get rid of. Rascal had to go through the treatment three times before he was clean. Only then could we start his heartworm treatment. To kill heartworms, the vet injects the dog with a poisonous medication. The dosage has to be carefully calibrated: too little means that not all the heartworms will die, but too much and you risk the dog's life. After the treatment, the dog has to be kept quiet for the four weeks it takes for the worms to die and for the dog to slough off the dead worms. If the dog is too active, the worm corpses could enter his lungs and cause a pulmonary embolism, resulting in death. Rascal, a young, energetic hound, living with two other young adult dogs, had to be kept in his crate in order to be kept quiet. Fostering Rascal took a lot of time and attention from us.

In all, Rascal had been with us for four months before he was finally able to be neutered and put up for adoption. During that time, Keith and Rascal bonded, much as Beowolf and I had. As Rascal and I were getting ready to go to our first adoption event, Keith walked in and asked me where we were going.

"Rascal and I are going to the adoption booth," I explained.

"You make sure you bring that dog back here afterwards."

"Sweetie, if he gets adopted, he'll probably go home with his new family."

Keith grumped in response. Partway through the event, he showed up and adopted Rascal. In the dog rescue community, when a foster family adopts the dog they were fostering, it is jokingly called a "foster fail." I have always argued that since I was the foster parent, and Keith was the adopter, Rascal's placement wasn't technically a fail.

By the time Cody came to live with us, Keith and I had left Tallahassee for Urbana, Illinois, leaving Robyn behind as a freshman at Florida State. Pepper was nine years old, Beowolf was eight, and Rascal was six.

Chapter 3

Foster Dog

Cody's steady, even gaze

WITHIN A FEW HOURS OF ARRIVAL, Cody had claimed spots in nearly every room, all of them on carpeted areas, behind or under pieces of furniture. These became his safe places. When anything frightened Cody, he would creep to his nearest safe spot and hide his head. He spent a lot of time examining the dust bunnies in the corners of our house.

Although Cody was obviously part yellow Lab, he didn't look like a purebred dog. His fur was softer than Labrador fur usually was. His ears seemed darker, too. Something about the placement of his ears was wrong for a Lab; I think they were more front-facing than Lab ears were supposed to be. His eyes were a surprisingly light shade of brown, much lighter than Pepper's eyes were. Finally, his tongue was blue. At least one vet who examined him was surprised to open Cody's mouth and see a blue tongue; the vet thought at first Cody wasn't getting enough oxygen and was cyanotic. A look at Cody's healthy pink gums helped the vet realize his mistake—Cody was evidently a Lab mix, but no one knew what he was mixed with.

The first time Cody went upstairs created an interesting dilemma for the cat. The whole pack and I walked into my bedroom for an afternoon nap. Clyde the cat was curled up and sleeping in the middle of the bed. He barely tolerated the dogs he knew; when he opened his eyes, he froze at the sight of a new dog. My pack, not knowing or caring that Clyde was having a panic attack, jumped up onto the bed while Clyde kept staring at Cody. Clyde realized he was on the bed with three dogs. In one movement, he went from reclining on the bed to hissing from the top of the headboard. I was going to rescue the kitty and carry him safely to the hallway, but the second I touched him, he unsheathed all his claws and tensed every muscle. I didn't need any new scars, so I told Clyde he was on his own. Clyde turned into a grey streak of lightning as he ran from the room, but Cody didn't even acknowledge the cat's existence. Instead, he curled up on the floor to sleep.*

Cody had so many needs that it was hard to pick out which ones to address first. House training would normally be at the top of my list, since I was determined not to live with an untrained pet, but I wasn't sure Cody could handle house training at all. It was a struggle to get him outside to the yard to potty. I had to snap a leash on him and walk him out, but he insisted on moving in his fearful crouch. The scars on his neck

---

* A couple of weeks after Cody's adoption, we temporarily added a fifth dog. A few days later, friends came to visit overnight with their cat. During their visit, Clyde disappeared. I don't know how he got out, but he'd apparently decided five dogs and two cats in the house were one cat too many.

were only a few months old, and I didn't know how tender they were or how much pain Cody felt if the leash pulled his collar. He cringed every time I reached toward him, especially when I touched his collar. Leash training therefore took precedence over house training. I ended up attaching a short handle to Cody's collar so I didn't have to constantly snap a leash on and off, but he didn't have to drag a 6' leash around with him. I was able to control his movements when needed without having to touch his neck.

Transitions were hard for Cody, whether they were changes in location or activity. I had taught long enough to know transitions were always difficult. The solution, whether with students or dogs, is to overlay a routine onto the transition so they know what to do at those times. I sang a special song for my young students at cleanup time. My middle and high school students had a routine to follow when they entered the classroom so by the time the bell rang, they were in their seats and ready to work. With three dogs, plus the occasional foster, feeding time had its own routine. Each dog would sit at their spot while I set their food in front of them, one by one. No one was allowed to eat until everyone had been served, and I gave the release command (free dog!). Cody would eat in his crate in my office until he was ready to join the other dogs in the kitchen at meal times.

Cody responded well to the structure of routines after only a few weeks. If I approached him with the phrase "Let's go," he knew I was leading him somewhere. He would immediately hop up from wherever he was hiding and approach me close enough for me to catch his handle.

After observing Cody for the first week, he seemed to me to be as much shy as fearful. He was interested in what was going on around him. He would watch everything that happened in the house from one of his many hiding places. He startled at every noise, but sometimes he would turn to track it and figure it out, not to run from it. He was always wary, but not always frightened.

On weekends or holidays, the dogs cuddled with me from the time I woke up to the time I got out of bed. I was in the process of earning a certificate in Teaching English as a Foreign Language. My college was on spring break when Cody moved into our home, so the next morning, Cody joined his first morning cuddle. The dogs and I were enjoying waking up slowly and taking care of the ears and tummies that needed petting to start the day. I was able to coax Cody to climb onto the bed with all of us. He lay beside me, stiff and trembling, and allowed me to pet and massage him all over for the first time. He didn't seem to like it, but he didn't run away either.

My bedroom soon became Cody's favorite place to be. During the day, I often found him at the top of the stairs, outside the closed bedroom door. There were many times I looked up the stairs and saw both Beowolf and Cody looking down at me, adorably expectant. One day I found them napping together in the hallway on the second floor while I had been working in my basement studio. Usually, Beo preferred to sleep on the sofa in the family room on the main floor, next to the basement door, so as to be closer to me, but I think Beo was intentionally keeping Cody company; Beowolf was that kind of dog.

I was willing to let Cody remove himself from the household during the day, but in the evenings, I didn't want Cody to separate himself from the rest of the pack while we were all in the family room together. He kept trying to sneak upstairs while I was cooking, and I kept going upstairs to bring him back down. He didn't want to leave his spot outside the bedroom door.

Once he tried crawling through the cat door to get into the bedroom. His head got stuck in the door momentarily; when he tried to pull his head back out, the plastic opening came out around his head. The incident alarmed him enough that he didn't try to go through the cat door again.

The pack was used to training foster dogs; we had fostered many dogs over three and a half years in Tallahassee before moving to Illinois. When anyone complimented my foster dogs' behavior at our monthly adoption booths, I always gave credit to Beowolf, Pepper, and Rascal. They taught new dogs the ropes by modeling appropriate behavior, and sometimes even encouraged or scolded the fosters. Even though it had been three or four years since we had had a foster, Beo and Rascal seemed to be trying to integrate Cody into the pack, while Pepper didn't care what Cody did as long as her dinner was on time. If I stood at the foot of the stairs and called Cody, Rascal raced up the stairs to where Cody was. He didn't bark at Cody, but he danced around him, running up and down a few steps, then going back to Cody to get the other dog to come with him. The only time I saw Cody's tail wag in that first week was a moment when he and Rascal touched noses. The wag was tentative, but it was definitely a wag.

If Cody had been a human, I would have said he had a low affect. That was the term educators used to describe kids who didn't react with outward emotion to things other kids responded to. That didn't mean he didn't feel things, only that he didn't show it. Understanding Cody meant looking for subtle, almost hidden, signs that showed what he was thinking and feeling. I thought he liked petting because of tiny little signs I picked up and interpreted. Or perhaps I just imagined them.

For Cody, just picking up his head indicated interest. Choosing proximity or approaching, even tentatively, was like raising his hand and saying, "Pick me," even if he ran away. If

Cody started to walk toward me or look at me when I was on the sofa, it meant he wanted to get up, even if he turned away when I invited him up. Once he was up there, if he put his head down near my hand, it was an invitation to pet him. I considered his interest, guarded as it was, as a positive sign. After all, the goal of fostering is to find the foster dog a permanent home. I was certain all Cody needed was one good bonding experience, and he'd be ready to join his forever family. I hoped the process would eventually be measured in months, not years.

To be sure, I made some mistakes along the way. I thought Cody might come along faster if he was forced to stay near me all day. It was a technique I had used successfully with previous fosters. Being close to me forced them to observe me in normal, daily activities. They also had a front-row seat to my interactions with the other dogs, which were generally warm and loving. I put a six-foot leash on Cody and attached the leash to my belt loop.

The result was an increase in the number of messes Cody left me to clean up, although he was only six feet away from me. After two days, I took the leash off and went back to the handle. I comforted myself with the realization that Cody was capable of letting me know if he was unhappy.

Training Cody was going to be a challenge because there was little I could offer him as an enticement or reward. He only permitted petting on his terms. He was frightened by my direct attention, so praise wasn't going to work. I also recognized Cody was not at all motivated by food. He frequently had leftovers in his dish. He rarely took treats from my hand—most often, I had to put the treat on the floor, and he would pick it up from there.

I incorporated lots of little gestures as part of Cody's rehabilitation. I tried to pet Cody under his chin when I could because that was one way to greet dominant dogs. I wasn't trying to tell Cody he was dominant, but rather to tell him I respected him. It also let me raise his head so he could see me, though he usually darted his eyes to the side to avoid making eye contact.

For my part, I made sure to avoid direct eye contact because it might have been too intimidating. When I wanted to smile at Cody or show approval, I looked at his ear and grinned. Showing my teeth in a smile and looking directly at him at the same time was too much like a dominance stare and baring my teeth, so I avoided it. If I wanted to talk to him, I used his name in every sentence. I knew he understood my tone and his name, but I didn't know if he understood anything else. I murmured things like "Cody is a good boy. I love Cody. Cody is a handsome dog," and so on, though I could have said things like, "Cody eats turtles. Cody wears clown shoes," and it wouldn't have mattered. All he was responding to at that point was my tone of voice and his name.

Dominant dogs tell subordinate dogs they are accepted members of the pack by holding their muzzles in their jaws. Since Cody was so passive, I tried to simulate that by stroking his muzzle with my cupped palm. If he had been less wary, I would have hugged his muzzle under my chin, which would have been much closer to how dogs communicate acceptance, but I felt that was too intimate right now.

One evening at bedtime, Cody started to sneak onto the dog cot next to the dresser from his chosen spot in front of the dresser. I turned my head to see what the sound was. When we made eye contact, he scurried back to his spot. Since I wanted Cody to use the cot, I took his leash handle and led him back to it, where he promptly lay down and curled into a ball. He kept his eyes open in case I was going to move again; his past life had left him suspicious of all humans. He fell asleep and spent the night there.

Cody made daily incremental improvement. I put a baby

gate at the bottom of the stairs so he couldn't go upstairs whenever he wanted, and was forced to learn to deal with the world in closer proximity. When I told the dogs to leave the bedroom every morning, Cody always needed an extra invitation, but I was able to stop leading him out anymore. After a few more weeks, when I told them to go downstairs first thing in the morning, Cody left the bedroom with the rest of the pack. "Outside" was a different matter; I had to find him and take him out. He started to walk into his crate in my office willingly at mealtimes and ate at least part of his meal every time. He was catching on to the routines. The evening routine of sitting with the family still took some convincing; he hopped off the couch the first chance he got. Overall, though, Cody was starting to fit in as part of our pack. Eventually, he was comfortable enough to start letting his inner dog out.

Unfortunately, his inner dog was part vampire.

The first thing Cody destroyed was a little stuffed cat toy that had been hanging from a dresser knob in my bedroom. I woke up one morning to find the toy no longer hanging and bits of stuffing on Cody's cot. That day, I bought Cody his own stuffed toy to play with. The next morning, I found Cody had taken one of Keith's slippers to his cot. It didn't look as if it had been chewed, though; Cody had apparently chosen to sleep with it all night.

Thus began the phase of Cody's rehabilitation I referred to as the "Vampire Dog." Cody was an aloof, watchful dog throughout the day, but he held himself back from interacting with the household. The other dogs seemed to overwhelm him with their noise and movement, though he didn't mind them when they were quiet. By night, though, Cody came alive.

We never knew what we would find when we woke up. Anything left on the floor was fair game for Cody to chew. I've never been tidy, but I learned to put things in drawers, the hamper, or the closet in order to preserve them, especially after he took a bite out of one of my sandals, leaving a crescent shaped bite mark in one of the leather straps. I also learned humans were harder to train than dogs. Keith insisted Cody had to learn not to chew our things, so he left his things out for Cody to resist. Cody didn't resist them. He chewed Keith's socks, underwear, and shoes regularly. Cody especially loved leather shoes—the more expensive the better.

Cody's most expensive nocturnal search and destroy mission forced me to change his environment. I woke up to a normal-appearing bedroom. After the morning ablutions, I reached toward my nightstand for my glasses. They weren't there. I looked on the dresser. No glasses. As I walked around the foot of the bed, I saw them, or something that used to be them. Cody had chewed my glasses overnight. The frame was twisted. One lens was cracked, and the other had popped out. One temple was torn off. I couldn't even put them on to drive to the optician. Fortunately, I had an old pair in a drawer.

While I was out getting new glasses made, I went to a local pet supply store and stocked up on dog toys, mostly soft ones. I cleared every surface in the bedroom and put away everything that was in Cody's reach. I placed some of the new toys on my nightstand, and put my new glasses in the nightstand drawer. While we slept, Cody took toys from the array of available toys, which I changed weekly. We would find one or all of them on the floor in the morning, sometimes along with bits of stuffing. While I wasn't all that fond of cleaning up dog-toy guts, I was glad to see that Cody was engaging in such typical doggy behavior, even if it was in the middle of the night.

Every night with Cody became an adventure. We were

often awakened during the night as Cody tried to entice the others into playing with him. We heard growls and barks on and off through the night. The bed bounced as Cody jumped on and off the bed. One night he jumped up on my side of the bed and ran across the bed (and us) before jumping off again. I woke up as he ran across my back. Keith, sleeping on his back, didn't fare as well; Cody landed right on his testicles. Fortunately, that never happened again; Keith's scream was deterrence enough for skittish Cody.

Generally, though, we were oblivious to Cody's activities while we slept. The few times he woke us, such as the incident above, he seemed to think we had awakened just to play with him. One night I roused when I heard him playing. He must have heard me waking up, because he jumped up on the bed, disturbing Pepper, who had been asleep at the foot of our bed. Cody barked at her and bowed, with his tail wagging, inviting her to play. Pepper reacted pretty much the way I would have to that kind of invitation, especially in the middle of the night: she just lifted her head, looked at Cody, and went back to sleep.

By the end of each night, our little vampire was on the bed. When Cody and I woke up, he would allow me to cuddle him. As he learned to accept the intimacy of cuddling, he discovered he liked having me scratch under his chin and on his muzzle, as well as rubbing his ears. He also lay on his side and let me spoon him to rub his tummy. Even though it wasn't the whole lying-on-his-back, legs-in-the-air tummy rub, it was a pretty trusting move on his part. I was genuinely touched the first time he rested his head on me as we lay on the bed together.

I learned Cody was at his most affectionate and playful with me first thing in the morning. His favorite game was helping me make the bed by preventing me from doing so. As I would fluff pillows and pull up sheets and blankets, he would grab them in his mouth or pounce on them. I never scolded him for his antics because I wanted to encourage him to play with me. This remained his habit for the rest of his life. In the morning, I could play with, cuddle, and pet him to my heart's content—and presumably his heart's as well. Once we left the bedroom, though, pets were limited and cuddles were nonexistent.

One evening, while I was lying in bed reading, Cody crept up to my nightstand to get one of his toys. He started giving it death shakes, throwing it in the air and catching it. He was having a wonderful time playing with it. I watched him from the corner of my eye, smiling at his fun. I was awake, the light was on, and Cody was playing.

The Vampire Dog phase was ending.

Within a few weeks after arriving at my home, Cody had learned to go into his crate when I asked him to, either by holding up his dish and telling him it was time to eat or by telling him "crate" because I had to lock him up so I could leave the house. He went up and down the steps by himself to go to bed or to go downstairs in the morning. I still had to walk him to the door to go outside, but it became a little easier once I realized he didn't like the noise of the other dogs barking to go out. I let them out first, then went to get Cody, and he allowed me to lead him to the door. He still didn't like being in the family room in the evenings, though he liked the petting. He even seemed to like watching TV. If I left him alone in my office and went into the family room, I could hear him whimpering for me, so I knew he wanted company. I couldn't quite figure out what it was he disliked about being in the family room. He still left as soon as he could, but he whimpered when he found himself alone in my office again.

As the Vampire Dog faded away, I started to see some

romping during the day. He actually initiated a romp with Beowolf one afternoon. They were bowing and posturing to each other, jumping and barking, with tails wagging. Cody chewed on Beo's hind foot a couple of times, which was one of Beo's usual tricks. I assumed Cody had learned that from watching Beo play with the rest of the pack. Little by little, we started to see more normal behavior from Cody. Keith nicknamed Cody "Pinocchi-dog," because he didn't behave like a 'real' dog, but we hoped someday he would transform into one.

Cody's behaviors reminded me of a child with autism. Let me state for the record: I am not suggesting Cody was autistic or that people with autism behave like dogs. Autism is a neurodivergent condition, whereas Cody's behavior was a learned coping mechanism he had developed from the abuse he had suffered early in his life. However, his behaviors were similar to someone whose sensory systems were overloaded or who didn't understand what was required in social interactions. When Cody was overwhelmed by too many people or dogs, changes in his environment, or too much noise, he would withdraw much as he had when he first arrived. He would literally turn his back on whatever had aroused his fear and wouldn't respond to anything, including soft voices, gentle pats, or treats. His withdrawals could be triggered by something as innocuous as a shopping bag being placed on the floor or a pile of mail on a table. He perceived anything new in his environment as a threat. Sometimes it took a bit of detective work to figure out what was upsetting him; often, I had to get on my hands and knees on the floor to be able to see what had triggered Cody's fear from his perspective. I learned to look at the world the way he did in order to help him.

Cody's progress was slow and steady, but not always linear. For example, one evening when all the dogs came in from outside, Cody stood in the middle of the pack and let them romp around him. He didn't jump or romp, though he did walk around Beo. He and Beowolf were mutually sniffing and posturing for play, but Cody stopped short of actually playing. His tail was wagging, and he had his mouth open in a doggy smile. It was the most affect I had seen from him up until that point. On the other hand, when our neighbors John and Stephanie came over to meet him, Cody stayed in a crouch and turned away from them. He allowed Stephanie to feed him a treat, but not John, and avoided all other contact and interaction with them. Life with Cody was often a dance with three steps forward, two steps back.

Keith's sales job took him out of town most of the week. It wasn't unusual for him to be away from Monday morning to Friday afternoon. During the year Cody came to live with us, Keith had been collecting the key cards from all his hotel stays and dropping them into a little gift bag in the kitchen. I wanted to see how many cards he collected in a one-year period as physical evidence of how much he was gone; I had begun to feel like the time we spent apart was starting to have a negative effect on our marriage. With Robyn living on her own and finishing her degree at Illinois State University, Keith and I were having to redefine our relationship. However, we were struggling to do that when we had so little time together.

Those nights when Keith was gone, the dogs and I slept alone in our bedroom. One Thursday, the dogs and I were just waking up from a late afternoon nap when Keith got home from yet another trip out of town. He opened the door to our bedroom. Cody was on the bed with me, already awake. As we heard the door open, he stood on the bed and started to bark like he was protecting his territory, with his hackles raised and his tail bristling. It was wonderful to see, even if I did have to call the dog off in order for Keith to enter his own bedroom.

Cody seemed to have decided that my husband was a stranger who invaded his territory from time to time. He seemed frightened of Keith and avoided him; Cody would always be more fearful around men than he was with women. In the early days, Cody wouldn't come up on the bed to sleep or cuddle when Keith was there, though he would hop up when Keith wasn't around. While Keith was home over a weekend, Cody wouldn't sleep or cuddle with us, but once Keith left town, Cody slept with me all night again. On the other hand, he did let Keith give him a little tummy rub, and he took pepperoni from Keith's hand while we were all downstairs. Little by little, he was overcoming his fear of Keith.

I kept the handle attached to Cody's collar most of the time. He still wasn't willing to walk from one place to another without me guiding him. However, bit by bit, he started to develop some independence. He walked upstairs at night with the other dogs, although there was sometimes a frantic edge to his attempts to get into the bedroom rather than just waiting for me to open the door. If he got impatient and ran back down the stairs, he came back up as soon as I called him. He went to his crate without an escort for meals or to be locked up when I had to leave.

I started testing him to see if he'd walk alone to the back door to go outside. He wouldn't come when I called, but walked easily if I took his handle and led him to the back door. He'd go into his fearful crouch again right as we got to the door, as if he expected something bad to happen when I opened the door, but he would walk outside by himself. Something about doorways seemed to frighten him, though I never figured out what it was or why.

After about a month, I decided to try walking Cody on a

leash outside the house. I walked him around the block using a harness so he wouldn't associate the leash with the scars from his previously embedded collar. I didn't know if the scars caused him any pain or discomfort, but they were horribly ugly to look at. The individual links were permanently imprinted in his flesh; his fur would never regrow to hide the scars. I thought they were likely to still be tender from the surgery several months earlier.

Much to my surprise, Cody walked easily on the leash. His head was up, and his ears were forward. He held his tail down, but not tucked. He sniffed the air and watched everything around him. He was startled by a lot of the noises, but he didn't seem frightened by them. He didn't go into a crouch, like he had done inside the house; he just turned quickly toward the source of the noise and backed away. It surprised me when he tried to lead me up several sidewalks toward the houses in our neighborhood. I wanted to encourage his curiosity, so I let him lead me up the sidewalk to a friend's house, and I rang the bell. Our friends came to the door, so he got to meet friendly strangers who petted him, including their six-month old daughter. Cody accepted their attention more easily than when he had met other strangers at home.

That evening, Cody added his voice to the chorus when the pack started to bark at a noise they'd heard outside. He ran outside with them to investigate. Beowolf always came up to me after the dogs sounded an intruder alert; I think he wanted reassurance he was still a Good Dog, and to get praise and approval for being a good protector. Cody came close, right behind Beo, and watched Beo get petted and praised, but Cody didn't let me do anything except boop his nose and tell him he was a good dog, too. He also wagged his tail a little and acted like he was going to play with Pepper—until she got overexcited. Cody couldn't handle Pepper's exuberance.

When Cody had been with us for about six weeks, I weighed the pros and cons of enrolling him in an obedience class. I couldn't decide if it was too soon to start working on formal commands or not. The interaction itself would have been good for Cody and would have strengthened our relationship, but it might have been too intimidating for the dog. He wasn't usually motivated by food, though he had begun to enjoy praise and petting. I thought he might work for pepperoni pieces well enough. The problem was I couldn't even get him to respond consistently to his name. I was afraid even working on "sit" might be an exercise in frustration for both of us. Much of training is based on the relationship between dog and trainer, but Cody and I didn't have that kind of relationship yet.

I went to the local Petsmart and spoke with the dog training instructor. I explained we were a foster family, and the rescue agency didn't have the money to pay for training. I told her Cody needed the socialization of the class much more than he needed the actual training; in fact, I wasn't sure he was ready for formal obedience training. She allowed Cody to attend a class that was just starting and had few dogs in it, waiving the fee since we didn't know if he was going to be able to learn anything.

I'm glad Cody "audited" his first obedience class because he spent most of it with his nose in a corner. When we arrived at Petsmart, Cody would walk straight back to the classroom area like he was a dog on a mission. His head was held high, and his gait was businesslike. No time to stop, sniff, or pee on anything. Time for class. And yet, Cody didn't seem to pay attention to anything once we gathered together. If there were extra chairs set up, Cody would hide behind or under them. He didn't always get to be where he wanted because he was on a leash, but nothing we did could get him to turn around and engage. As far as formal learning was concerned, we didn't get any further than eliciting eye contact when I said his name.

However, Cody came out of his shell when attrition dropped the class down to only one other dog. With one dog in the class, Cody was willing to interact with him, but they didn't have an opportunity to play with each other; this was school, after all. Cody's presence was valuable to the other dog because Cody created a distraction which the other dog needed to learn to ignore, while the other dog created learning opportunities for Cody just by existing in the same space. At the end of the class, Cody didn't graduate, but I thought he had gained something important by attending. He was starting to make his own choices.

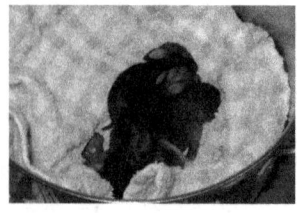

The baby bunnies Cody and Beowolf rescued

One night in May, 2006, when Cody had been with us about two months, I went to the back door to call the pack into the house. Pepper and Rascal came in right away, but Beowolf was nosing around in the grass, while Cody was sitting straight and tall, refusing to budge. This was the same dog who still crawled on his belly to go from place to place in front of humans he didn't know. I couldn't figure out what had happened to give Cody the courage to resist me. He looked me in the eye when I told him "let's go," and didn't twitch. I left the dogs outside a little while longer. When I returned to call them in, both dogs were sitting up ramrod straight and wouldn't respond. It wasn't like Beo to disobey, but it was absolutely out of character for Cody to look me in the eye at all, much less holding this steady, even gaze as he made it clear he wasn't moving. I didn't want to frighten Cody, but I literally had to chase both dogs into the house so we could all go to bed.

The next morning, when I let the dogs out, I heard barking from Pepper and Rascal, the two who had come into the house willingly the night before. I looked out the window and saw that Pepper and Rascal were barking at both Cody, who was sitting at attention in the same spot, and Beowolf, who was again nosing and pawing at something in the grass. This time I went outside to investigate. In the daylight, I could see what was happening. Cody was guarding a litter of newborn baby bunnies, while Beowolf was trying to push an errant bunny back to the nest. Another one had died, presumably overnight. The barking dogs wanted to eat or play with the new squeaky toys.

Some dumb bunny had given birth in our nice, safe, fenced-in yard, only to discover it was home to four dogs. She then took off, leaving her babies behind, and never returned. Fortunately, Beowolf, being a dog who loved children and other small animals, was not going to let Pepper and Rascal do anything to hurt them. It was a pleasant surprise that Cody, for all that he was afraid of almost everything, was Beo's ally in protecting those little baby bunnies.

I carefully nestled the babies in a bowl I had lined with a dishtowel and took them to the University of Illinois College of Veterinary Medicine's Wildlife Clinic. I knew they would get the best care possible. I like to think that there are four cotton-tails and their descendants in the countryside around Urbana that owe their lives to two big-hearted dogs.

I was proud of my boys. I was especially proud of Cody, even though he hadn't obeyed me. Cody had seen two choices and made the one that was right, even when I, in my ignorance, had told him to do something else. He had looked straight into my eyes and stood his ground.

Cody started making a lot of progress, albeit in fits and starts. He played with the other dogs more frequently. All four of them would bark and romp together, jump on each other, bow, and otherwise play. They only did it in my office, though, and only when I was in there with them. When I wanted Cody to go outside, I only had to walk him past the stairs to the point where he could see the back door and command "outside." Once he saw the door, he walked by himself and waited for me to open the door. He still crouched by the door, but not as much; it was more of a bend than a crawl. There was even one time when I announced "outside" to the pack in general, and Cody trotted out with the others.

When I was at home by myself one Friday, I had the back door open all day to let in the lovely late spring weather. Cody went in and out by himself at will. Once he'd crossed that threshold, both literally and figuratively, he was able to continue doing it. Having the door open seemed to give Cody a sense of freedom to explore in safety.

We also had training sessions now and then. During these sessions, I would put the dogs through their obedience commands as a review. All of them knew how to "sit." Beowolf and Pepper also knew "down." Pepper had had the most training because she had needed it the most. Along with "heel," "stay," and "wait," she had learned what we called "The Nose Trick." I would balance a cookie on her muzzle and command "wait." When I gave her the signal, she would toss the cookie up and catch it in her mouth.

People ask me how I taught Pepper to catch the cookie. The

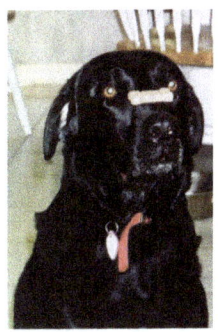

Pepper doing her "nose trick"

truth is she taught herself; I only taught her to wait for the release command with the cookie on her nose. The motivation to catch it came from Beowolf and Rascal, who would grab the cookie before Pepper could get to it if she casually tossed it to the floor. Competition can be a great motivator.

To start a training session, all I had to do was walk over to the cookie jar, which held dog biscuits. Beowolf, Pepper, and Rascal would come running in, while Keith brought Cody in. I gave the others biscuits as rewards for following my commands, but I offered Cody pieces of pepperoni just to try to get him to accept them in the kitchen, while on the leash, and from my hand. He was reluctant to accept the treats, but he did finally take two or three. Imagine having to teach a dog to eat meat! The funny thing was that for all that Cody cowered and trembled while Keith held his leash handle and I tried to give him treats, as soon as we let him leave, he sauntered away at a slow and casual pace, looking proud of himself.

There was another day when there was a lot of dominance mounting going on. In fact, Beowolf and Rascal briefly crossed the line from playing to fighting, which seemed to scare Cody. The noteworthy thing was that Cody and Rascal were taking turns mounting each other. Yes, Cody was actually mounting Rascal to show dominance. At the same time, he wasn't passively allowing Rascal to mount him. It was an amazing moment for me as an observer.

I decided it was time to move Cody's crate from my office into the family room/kitchen; I thought he was ready to have his den in the room where most of the household activity took place. He started choosing to go into his crate for a few minutes at a time. He was already used to eating in his crate and being in there when no one was home. Unfortunately, Cody apparently had a strong dislike of being in his crate with the door closed on him. Unbeknownst to me, he spent a lot of time while he was locked in the crate chewing on the bars. As a result, he wore down his front teeth, top and bottom, all the way to the gum line. The stumps of his teeth were still visible, but didn't seem to cause him any pain. I realized I needed to work on giving him the skills he needed to be left alone without crating him: being completely house trained and only chewing his own toys, not ours. His greatest temptation was chewing on things made of fabric; stuffed animals, socks, and curtains were especially vulnerable.

Cody showed me in his body language that he was recovering from his past. He started to walk a little taller, with less of a crouch than before. I even saw him lift his leg outside when he peed. That might not seem like a big deal, or even a thing worth noting, but low ranking or submissive male dogs usually urinate in a crouch like puppies do; that had been Cody's habit since his arrival. Cody's lifted leg showed he wasn't automatically submissive anymore. I had the distinct impression Cody had emerged as the middle ranking male dog, with Rascal still at the bottom. I couldn't work out how that had happened, but then again, I wasn't a dog.

After a few months of living with us, Cody walked from place to place in the house and only rarely needed to be led by his handle. I was soon able to remove it from his collar altogether. Cody walked with his head up, and although he might have his tail down, it wasn't tucked anymore. He sometimes walked with a slight crouch, but generally he was pretty straight-legged. He wouldn't come to me for social interaction if I called him, but he would sneak up on the bed or creep beside my chair, and enjoyed being petted once he was there. He still disappeared like a shot if I made eye contact. That meant I couldn't look at him and call his name, or pat a space next to me and signal for him to come. He was still distrusting of humans, even the one he knew best.

After Cody had lived with us for four months, Patty and I decided he was ready to be adopted. He had gained all the basic behaviors and manners a dog needed to live with humans. What he needed from that point on was patience. He was still skittish and fearful, but only time in a loving household was going to cure him. It was time to find his forever family and home.

The first person to interview Cody was our neighbor Stephanie's mother. While she knew Cody's history and had heard about him from her daughter, she wasn't prepared for how needy he was. Cody hid under a table in my office when she arrived, so she had to get on the floor to see him. He wouldn't respond to her or take a treat from her. She decided he needed more care than she could give at the time.

Since Patty was the director of the animal rescue group that had placed Cody with me, she often heard from prospective adopters looking for dogs. One family struck her as having the patience and love to deal with a dog with special needs. Given how badly the previous interview had gone, we decided to meet at a park. Perhaps throwing Cody a little off-balance would make it less likely that he would try to hide, just as he walked better on a leash outside the house compared to inside. Cody behaved much more appropriately being in a strange place, but he still ignored the family trying to meet him. His behavior showed them just how much care and patience Cody would need if he was ever going to be "normal." The family was pleasant and would have given Cody a loving home, but he was needier than they could handle.

Patty and I talked over the situation. Cody was ready for

adoption, but it didn't seem anyone was interested in adopting him given his ongoing needs. In the month he had been available, only those two families had wanted to meet him. It was unlikely we would find his forever home soon; I might have to foster Cody for months or even years before we found the right match. Patty indicated she thought he'd already found the right match, and by the time I got home, I realized she was right. I already knew all of Cody's quirks. I was able to provide him with the therapeutic environment he needed. More than that, I loved him. Five months after he walked into my house, Cody became part of my family and my life. He became my dog.

(That, by the way, is another foster fail. I wish all my failures had turned out so well.)

Chapter 4

Illinois

Karma and Cody

OVER THE NEXT TWO YEARS, Cody continued to make slow, steady progress. Another dog temporarily joined our pack a few weeks after Cody's adoption. Karma was a seven-year-old Shetland sheepdog whose life was severely limited by her fears. She lived in her owner's bedroom, only going outside to relieve herself. She trembled and barked whenever someone came to the door. She hid under the bed. She had become so difficult to handle that her fur was matted and her nails overgrown because Karma refused to get into the car for grooming appointments. Karma's owner was an elderly woman who loved the dog, but didn't know how to help her. I offered to take Karma into my home and try to train her—or, more likely, have the other dogs train her.

The first thing I did was take Karma to a groomer. I knew

she would feel more comfortable without the mats pulling on her skin. When her nails were trimmed, they would no longer distort her paws into painful, almost crippling forms. With cute little red bows in her fur, Karma looked adorable. I think she knew it; she walked with her head a little higher after leaving the groomer. I also took Karma to our vet, where she got a dental cleaning and treatment for a skin condition.

Karma's Pup Tent

At home, I attached a handle to her leash as I had with Cody, but it was mostly to prevent her from being able to escape and hide; she was otherwise fine walking on a leash. Karma's instinct was to hide in Cody's crate, so I ended up having to leave his empty crate locked so Karma couldn't get in there. Instead, I got Karma a small nylon crate with zippers; I called it her pup tent. I had to zip it closed when I didn't want her in there.

There was one amusing incident with Karma and Cody's crate. Our neighbors came by with their now ten-month-old daughter. Beowolf was fascinated by Evie, as he was with all children, but Evie only had eyes for Karma. Karma had never been exposed to children, so I sat back to watch what would happen. Karma tried to run from this little creature, but the creature kept coming after her. Karma's patience was starting to run out, especially when Evie seemed determined to twist off Karma's nose. In order to protect that nose—and Evie's fingers—I let Karma go into Cody's crate. From inside the crate, Karma watched her tormentor, while Evie stood at the front, trying to figure out the latch.

Cody recognized Karma as a kindred spirit, and became her mentor much as Beowolf had done with him. For the six weeks Karma was with us, she and Cody were inseparable. During the day, they played together. At night, they slept together. Both of them were intimidated by the noise of the other dogs and found comfort in being together in quiet enjoyment.

It was a good reality check to realize Cody had grown enough to be able to help another dog learn the same skills he had struggled with. He modeled for Karma the routines that he had recently mastered. I don't know enough about canine communication to explain exactly how he guided her, but I noticed that she looked to him whenever she was unsure, just as he had once looked to Beowolf.

I wasn't as appreciative of their friendship when I discovered the two dogs had joined forces and stolen a small quilted pillow from Robyn's room, carried it downstairs, and disemboweled it. I didn't know they were up to mischief until I saw the pillow innards strewn all over my office. Perhaps I should have been suspicious of the silence, except those two dogs were always quiet.

Karma became the top-ranking female dog, mostly because Pepper was too much of a free spirit to compete for dominance. Cody was the second ranked male dog. Karma and Cody therefore competed for the second-in-command spot after Beowolf. They developed their own ways of communicating and settling their differences. Karma, perhaps imitating Baby Evie, would bite Cody on the nose when he did something she didn't like. Cody, in turn, would complain to Karma about what she had done in barks and howls. Their conversations over who was higher in rank were amusing to hear, except in the middle of the night; Karma was going through her own Vampire Dog phase.

By the time she left "Karma's Kanine Boot Kamp," Karma had learned to respond to voice commands, walk outside, bark to protect her pack, and play like a dog with other dogs. She remained timid, but her horizons had expanded beyond one bedroom. Overall, she was a happier dog. Cody, for his part, had shown Karma what being a dog meant, something I hadn't been sure he knew himself.

As long as he knew what to expect, Cody seemed like any other dog. His days of wearing a handle were now long gone. He was fully integrated into our pack and family. He no longer stood on the fringes of the pack, watching the other dogs have fun; he was right in the middle of whatever was going on. When we had our annual latke party for Chanukah in December, 2006, Cody stood in the middle of the room, all the activity going on around him, with a big, goofy grin on his face. He wasn't interacting with any of the guests, but he was obviously enjoying the party. He was almost unrecognizable as the quivering mass of dog flesh we had first met nine months earlier.

Being out in public was hard for Cody, which made it hard for us when he was along. Although he was always on a leash when we left the house, he was likely to try to run away if something nearby startled him. Even though Cody needed continued work on socialization with humans and adapting to strange situations, we weren't always sure he was ready for the lessons. When a dog feels fear or anxiety, they aren't able to learn something new. We tended to avoid taking Cody anywhere unless we could be certain the setting was somewhat controlled.

One of the places that Cody enjoyed going was our daughter Robyn's apartment. Robyn, by then 22 years old, had a Boston terrier named Monkey who was about a year younger than Cody. Monkey's nickname was Mimou (*my-moo*), the Greek word for "monkey." Mimou was everything Cody was not—active, brave, dominant, and assertive—and Cody seemed to worship her. When they were together, at our house or hers, Monkey would try to mount Cody in a dominance display. She was too short to reach Cody, so he would obligingly lie on the floor for her. Mimou usually started at Cody's tail and humped her way along his body until she got to his head. Cody just lay there and grinned as she did it. She walked around to his tail and did it all again. The two were such good friends that they always recognized each other when they were reunited, no matter how many months or years it had been.

By the time 2006 had ended, Keith had collected close to 200 hotel key cards, each one representing at least one night apart. We struggled to connect with each other when we were together, even though we spoke by phone nearly every day. We started to see a marriage counselor. I learned that Keith saw the collection of hotel key cards as a sign I blamed him for being gone, even though I had never considered it was his fault his job required him to travel. I also learned that Keith had frequently told me what he thought I wanted to hear rather than share his own opinions honestly. For nearly as long as I could remember, I had wanted to live abroad and have the opportunity to learn about another culture by being a part of it. Keith had told me he agreed with the concept beginning when Robyn was in preschool, but he always had a reason we should put it off for another year. I learned in counseling that he had never had any intention of living abroad. I felt betrayed and hurt by his dishonesty and wondered what else he had been dishonest about.

While I had been on disability, I had added a certificate in Teaching English as a Foreign Language (TEFL) on top of my master's degree in education. I had been teaching ESL part time and doing some private tutoring for a few years, and I wanted to combine my professional training with my interest in living abroad.

My first attempt at returning to full-time employment since going on disability—teaching special education resource at a high school—had not gone well. The job of being a special education teacher had changed in the 10 years since I had last been a classroom teacher. The demands of the job included everything a regular classroom teacher had to do, plus enough paperwork and case management duties to fill another half- or full-time position. I had had to leave the position I had started in August, 2007, at the end of the first semester in order to preserve my mental health. I was looking for another job when I asked Keith if it was okay with him if I taught overseas for a semester, roughly four to five months. I pointed out we were already apart much of the time. Keith agreed to my proposal. Secretly, I hoped Keith would miss me while I was gone, realize he was taking me for granted, and become eager to rejuvenate our marriage. In February, 2008, I went to China to teach English as a Second Language (ESL) at a university in Inner Mongolia for one semester.

The dogs, of course, stayed behind. Keith took care of them, with Robyn and Monkey filling in when Keith was out of town. Cody seemed somewhat depressed, as he always was when we were separated, but he was in familiar surroundings with people and dogs who loved him. He may have eaten a little less than normal, but he remained healthy. By the time I returned in July, 2008, Cody's pack included Robyn and Monkey.

Shortly after I returned from China, I learned that, rather than missing me, Keith had found his life had continued quite well without me. We decided our 29-year marriage had run its course. We legally separated on August 1, 2008, and I moved into the guest bedroom until I could make other arrangements. Robyn was an adult at that point, living on her own, and planning a wedding for September. The only custody arrangements we had to make were for the dogs. There was no question about custody of Beowolf, Rascal, and Cody; those dogs had shown their preference for one or the other of us. Pepper could have gone with either of us, but I ended up finding an apartment that only allowed two pets per unit. That decided the issue: Beowolf and Cody would move out with me, while Pepper and Rascal would stay with Keith.

At about the same time that we were making these decisions, I noticed there was a lump on Beowolf's eyelid. His vet suggested removing it because it could scratch his cornea if left in place. As she performed the surgery, she noted that the growth wasn't a cyst, as we had thought; it was a tumor of some sort. The lab performed a biopsy and reported that it was malignant; Beowolf had cutaneous lymphoma. The treatment, which wouldn't have been particularly effective, would have made him feel worse than the cancer itself would have. Beo wouldn't have had the understanding a human would have had that feeling sick was part of getting well. He would be miserable, and he would still die. He probably only had a few months left.

I was devastated by the news. Beowolf was 10 years old, which wasn't a bad lifespan for a large dog, but I had hoped to have more time with him. He was and is my forever dog, a special dog who will always have a home in my heart. No other dog has been the companion Beowolf was, though Cody came close. I had just lost my husband and my marriage. My daughter had married and moved 600 miles away to Baltimore. Now I was going to lose my best friend as well.

The dogs and I moved into our new apartment on October 1, 2008. I had to walk the dogs three or four times every day since there wasn't a fenced area they could play in, and I was able to observe Beowolf's deteriorating condition as the boys explored their new environment. Beowolf grew weaker, thinner, and greyer week by week. He hardly played with Cody anymore—he just didn't have the energy. I decided to take them to the dog park, which was about a mile from our new home, so Cody could play with the other dogs.

Cody was cautious at the dog park, even though he'd been

there before. He went to areas where there weren't any other dogs so he could sniff around alone. When a human approached, Cody moved away, hiding behind the trees or under the nearest unoccupied bench.

Beowolf, in contrast, was greeted by the other dogs as an alpha, which hadn't happened on our previous visits. Beo had always been a relatively submissive dog. Other than within our own pack, he was always a follower rather than a leader. However, based on how the other dogs responded to Beo, something had obviously changed. The closest analogy I can think of in the human world is Beowolf had become an Elder. He wouldn't have been able to assert his dominance through physical intimidation, but the other dogs looked up to and respected him. At one point, some of the younger dogs were roughhousing and crossed the line into fighting. Beowolf let out a single loud, sharp woof. The dogs stopped fighting immediately, and all the dogs, not just those that were fighting, came running over to lick Beo's muzzle. Well, not *all* the dogs; Cody just watched.

Beowolf celebrated his eleventh birthday in November, 2008. It was hard to watch his decline, but it was harder to think of living without him. I went to the vet's office about every other week. We had lots of frank discussions about euthanasia, but I simply wasn't ready to let Beowolf go. The vet was compassionate with both my struggles and Beo's illness. She assured me that Beowolf would tell me when it was time.

He did.

One Saturday afternoon in early December, Beowolf was barely able to go outside. Climbing up on the sofa beside me seemed to be the only thing he had energy for. I wasn't sure he would survive the weekend; I wasn't even sure he would survive the day. I sat beside him and petted him. I read *Dog Heaven* by Cynthia Rylant to him over and over, as often as he wanted to listen to it. It was a children's picture book about the afterlife for dogs, a place where dogs could run without ever getting tired, where treats grew everywhere, and where there were people to love and pet them. I wouldn't have thought that looking at a picture book would mean anything to a dog, but Beowolf seemed fascinated by the book. He would listen attentively as I read it, even seeming to look at the pictures. Beo enjoyed watching movies; maybe he was looking at the book. Maybe I was projecting something human onto Beowolf, but he seemed to find comfort in it. Perhaps it was just my voice that was comforting to him.

On Monday, Beowolf was still alive, so I called the vet's office and told her it was time. We had already decided the procedure would be done at home. One of the vet techs who had seen Beo at our frequent office visits had asked to be with Beowolf at the end, but between her schedule and the vet's, it would be Thursday before they could do it. When Thursday came, I set up Beo's cot in the living room. He crawled onto it and never crawled off.

Keith was going to bring Pepper and Rascal with him to my apartment. We had learned from having so many foster dogs that the remaining dogs did better when they knew what had happened to the missing dog. When fosters got adopted or picked up away from our house, our dogs looked for the foster to return. They wandered around the house and stood at the front door, whining as they did so. When the adoptive parents came to our house to get the foster, the dogs didn't seem disturbed at all. We agreed that Cody, Pepper, and Rascal deserved the chance to say goodbye to Beowolf.

Keith and the dogs arrived at my apartment at about the same time as Stephanie, Beowolf's "girlfriend." Stephanie and her husband were our backdoor neighbors, and on the rare occasion that Beo escaped out the front door, he would go to Stephanie's house. They mutually adored each other. It was a sweet relationship, and when I knew Beowolf's life was ending, I invited Stephanie to be part of our celebration of him.

While we waited for the vet and her assistant to arrive, Keith read Beowolf's book to him. It was the only time the whole day that Beowolf lifted his head off the cot; I thought he wanted to look at the pictures. Other than that, Beowolf lay still on his cot while the humans and dogs of his pack attended to him.

The procedure was quick and painless for Beowolf; the rest of us felt so much pain that it was spilling out of our eyes. Cody, Pepper, and Rascal sniffed Beowolf as he lay still on the cot. The vet wrapped Beowolf in a blanket and took him with her; he would be sent out for cremation. The other dogs didn't seem distressed at all. Rascal even climbed up on the empty cot. I felt an irrational anger at them for not being more upset. I didn't want them to hurt, but I wanted them to understand why I was hurting. Stephanie and Keith left soon after the vet, along with Pepper and Rascal.

Beowolf died on December 11, 2008. For the first time, Cody and I were on our own.

Life was not good to me in the first few months after Keith and I separated. I went through so many losses in such a short period of time that I didn't have time to recover from one loss before the next would pile on. In August, of course, my marriage ended. In September, Robyn got married and left Illinois for Maryland, where my father, stepmother, and three of my four siblings lived. In November, I started having what appeared to be menstrual bleeding, except I was already post-menopausal. The bleeding became so heavy I soaked through a tampon in 30 minutes. I ended up going to the emergency room, where I had to have a blood transfusion of two units. I also had to have a D & C—Dilation and Curettage—in which the lining of my uterus was scraped out while I was under anesthesia. It didn't stop the bleeding, but at least it slowed down.

Two weeks after that procedure, I lost Beowolf. Two weeks after Beo's death, I celebrated my 50th birthday alone; I didn't see another human the entire day. One of the problems with a Christmas birthday is everyone else is busy celebrating, so birthdays get overlooked. I was still bleeding throughout January, so I called the gynecologist's office to ask if the bleeding would ever stop. By the time I went in for the next appointment, the bleeding had finally stopped, but the doctor told me I needed a hysterectomy. He tried to get a tissue sample while I was in the office, but the procedure was too painful for me without anesthesia. I had to have another D & C in February to provide tissue samples prior to surgery. In March, I had my uterus removed. Robyn came back to Urbana to take care of me for the first week after surgery, and my mother flew in from North Carolina to be with me for the second week.

In April, I gave a talk at a conference of the Illinois Rehabilitation Association held locally. The professionals in attendance worked with clients struggling with alcohol or substance abuse, stroke, or disability. Several fields were represented, including mental health counselors, physical therapists, vocational trainers, and a variety of health care workers. My topic was an insider's view of suicidal ideation.

I had been diagnosed with depression when I was 30. Most of my life had been colored by chronic, mild depression with intermittent periods of severe depression. I had often considered suicide as a way to escape the psychological pain that was part of my life every day. Even as I was sharing my most intimate struggles with my audience, I was telling them how much better I was coping compared to past events. I listed everything that had happened in the previous eight months, adding that I was proud of myself that the losses and dispossessions hadn't pushed me into a deep depression. I heard a voice in the audience say the events I was sharing would have made anyone depressed, let alone someone with a history of depression. I got a round of applause for my mental health and strength.

A lot of the credit for my fortitude goes to Cody. He was my only companion for the first month after Beowolf died. He was the foundation upon which my recovery rested, just as I was his. I feared that meant we were both building our lives on shaky foundations. Still, with no one else to turn to, we learned to turn to each other. Cody seemed more tolerant and forgiving of my need to be close to him. He allowed more hugs and stayed when he might have run and hidden even a few weeks earlier. For my part, I saw Cody was lonely while I was at work all day, so I decided to adopt another dog.

After Clyde had moved out, I had told Beowolf I would get him a grey kitten and name it Grendel. He would have loved a little kitty to play with, but the time was never right to bring a new baby into the household. Therefore, when I adopted a grey cairn terrier to keep Cody company, I named her Grendel.

Grendel was the perfect companion for Cody. She was older than he was, about seven to nine years old compared to Cody's five, but active and affectionate, with lively black eyes. As a pet, Grendel left a little to be desired; she was never 100% house trained in the time she lived with me. However, as a friend and companion for Cody, she was excellent. She and Cody wrestled together, neither one minding the difference in their sizes. They enjoyed curling up together for naps, but they both enjoyed time alone as well. They also worked together to destroy things in my home, like pulling the stuffing out of my comforter. Grendel was a little imp, and Cody happily followed along.

Grendel was also instrumental in helping me with a young girl I tutored a couple of years later. The second-grade child had an Autism Spectrum Disorder, and was in a classroom with about seven other students with ASD. Her parents had both grown up in Asia; her younger sister was bilingual. The girl herself was technically bilingual, but she wasn't able to express herself well in either language. I took Grendel along with me to a lesson at the girl's house to see if talking to or about the little dog might elicit communication from her.

Grendel was happy to be held and petted by the little girl. She tolerated some rough handling as the girl learned how to interact with a dog appropriately. The girl dictated a story for me to write down, using complete sentences to describe the little dog. Her story about Grendel provided the materials for several lessons. At every lesson thereafter, she asked if Grendel could come back. We worked out ways for her to earn visits from Grendel, proving that the sweet little dog with the bright eyes was a natural therapy dog.

Chapter 5

Baltimore

Cody in his training vest and Grendel

WHEN SCHOOL LET out for the summer, I relocated to Maryland to be near Robyn and the rest of my family. Keith and I had tried repeatedly to move closer to my parents and siblings in the Baltimore-Washington area, but we had never been able to find jobs for both of us in the same location. Now that I was alone, I moved without first having a job in hand. In order to move, I had to put almost all my belongings in storage; I could only take what would fit in my car. Until I could get a job and find a place to live, I would live temporarily with my father and stepmother. They might have tolerated my moving in with a cat, but dogs were not welcome in their home. Keith was willing to have Cody stay with him until I was settled in my own place. Robyn, recently separated from her soon-to-be-ex-husband, was willing to let Grendel stay with her.

Unfortunately, Robyn didn't consult with Monkey. Having a pack with only two small, dominant, female dogs was a bad idea. Either Grendel annoyed Mimou so much that Mimou started leaving messes in the house, or Grendel forgot everything she'd ever learned about toileting, which admittedly wasn't much. Either way, someone was making it impossible to walk barefoot in Robyn's house, so Grendel had to find another temporary home. Fortunately, my mother, who was still living in North Carolina, agreed to care for Grendel.

I spent most of that summer looking for work, a task I was sadly all too familiar with. I was chronically between jobs. I had always had trouble keeping a job throughout my career. I never stayed anywhere more than two years. Supervisors had talked to me about "staff perception," that I wasn't a team player, that I was arrogant, or that I didn't get along with others, though they rarely had anything negative to say about my actual teaching. The accumulated weight of not-quite-fitting-in would reach a critical mass after about two years, and I would decide not to stay. No supervisor or colleague had ever been able to cite a specific incident to explain any of their vague concerns or to indicate a pattern of any sort, so I was never able to change my behavior. I had started therapy way back in 1988 originally to deal with my social incompetence, but it never surfaced in one-to-one situations like therapy. Twenty years later, I still didn't know what I was doing that impeded my success.

I wasn't opposed to teaching abroad, but the positions I was offered didn't excite me enough to be willing to leave everyone I knew behind. I didn't want to teach at a police academy in Tajikistan or have to dress 'modestly' to teach in Oman. However, public school systems were notorious for hiring new teachers up until the day school starts. I decided to wait and see what turned up. At that point, I was certified to teach both Special Education and English Language Arts. I thought of myself primarily as an English or ESL teacher, but principals only wanted to talk to me about hard-to-fill special education positions. I ended up being hired to teach "Social Studies Inclusion" at a middle school.

Being a Social Studies inclusion teacher should have put me in a social studies classroom as a co-teacher with a teacher certified in Social Studies. The teaching would become collaborative, with both of us working from our strengths, so the needs of all the students were better met, regardless of disability or need. At least, that was how the job was presented to me and why I accepted it.

As soon as I had a signed contract, I applied for a mortgage on a house I had fallen in love with—a 1920 bungalow in West Baltimore. It had been updated and modernized, but the original house had been left mostly intact. I moved in late September, 2009, and got all my possessions out of storage. Keith drove the truck from Illinois for me, with Cody, Pepper, and Rascal in the front seat. Keith now shared his life with a man who didn't like dogs, so I had offered to take custody of Pepper and Rascal again. I drove to North Carolina to pick up Grendel from my mother. Having all my fur babies back with me made my house into a home.

Cody had become more adaptable about new places, as long as the people he loved were with him. While Pepper and Rascal were busily exploring and Grendel cuddled on my lap, Cody was happy to reclaim his old place on the sofa. We all settled in for a long, happy life together.

I wish it had happened that way.

There are moments in life that seem inconsequential when they happen, yet which haunt us in later years. One such moment occurred when I went to the school system's administrative offices to sign my contract. I ran into Wayne, the recruiter who had sent me for the interview that led to the job offer. Wayne was a particularly caring educator and administrator, now working in the Human Resources office in teacher recruitment. While he had referred me to interview for the position I had accepted, he knew I would have preferred an English or ESL position. Wayne told me he had just received the paperwork for an opening for a full-time ESL teacher. I could have chosen to pursue that opening, but I felt obligated to honor the agreement I had with the school that had hired me. If only I had realized the school would not be equally honorable in their treatment of me. If only I had pursued that ESL opportunity. If only...

The theory behind the inclusion model was that most students with special needs could receive instruction from the same subject area specialist who taught the kids without special needs. The special ed kids needed support from a learning specialist, a.k.a. a special ed teacher, who could develop alternate materials or assignments for the students that drew on the students' strengths. By placing the special ed teacher in the same room while the content specialist was teaching, the special ed teacher could respond immediately to anyone who seemed to need help. In that way, the student didn't have to sacrifice a class period at another time for a Resource class. It also allowed for flexible grouping, so if there were other students who were having trouble, they could get assistance, too, even if they hadn't been identified as having a special need.

My duties should have been things like monitoring the students' behavior so the social studies teacher could teach without disruption. I wouldn't necessarily be planning lessons, but I would have to prepare materials in advance. I might rewrite passages from the text to make them easier for students to understand or record myself reading aloud so students could hear as well as see the text. I could come up with alternate assignments for students so their learning problems didn't interfere with showing the teacher how much they had learned. During tests or quizzes, I might be called on to take the students who were easily distracted into a separate room. If necessary, I could read the test to the students and even write down their dictated answers. In theory, 'social studies inclusion' was a way to connect the students with the information by changing the demands the classroom placed on them.

In practice, however, I was the social studies teacher for three sections of World Geography per day; other special ed teachers came to my classroom to do the inclusion portion. I didn't realize how wrong the situation was until the parent open house. As I wrote a brief biography to introduce myself to the parents, I suddenly realized I was the only social studies teacher for all these kids who didn't have any special educational needs. There was at least one special ed kid in every class, which was how the administration had justified placing me there, but I wasn't certified to teach social studies. I'd never even taken a course in how to teach social studies. I didn't know the information I was responsible for teaching to the students; I was teaching world geography without ever having taken a geography course. If I had been a parent at that open house and had learned my child's social studies teacher didn't know anything about the subject and wasn't certified to teach it, I would have been furious.

I think I hated that job more than any other I've ever had. I shouldn't have accepted it in the first place, because it was middle school and I'm not a middle school teacher. I love early childhood, roughly age 4 to 8, and I enjoy working with high school and college-aged students. I even like teaching adults. I just can't deal effectively with middle school kids, especially in a herd. If the job had been anything like the description, I would have been okay as a teacher, but not great. However, since I ended up in a job I wasn't qualified for, it was a nightmare.

The administration was not supportive; they were more concerned with protecting themselves than with making sure I was an appropriate match for the position or the students were being well served. There were people with the authority to tell me what to do who didn't have the credentials or qualifications for their positions; making matters worse, I did have the appropriate credentials. Half of my planning time was taken away to add a fourth Geography class to my load, but the special ed administrative duties I was expected to fulfill weren't lessened. I had previously received disability payments because of my depression, which was worsened by stress. By November, 2009, I asked the school district for accommodations under the Americans with Disabilities Act (ADA). When they couldn't accommodate me at that school, they allowed me to transfer to another middle school, this time as an English teacher.

My new principal resented having to accept me as a transfer. She had wanted to hire the daughter of the head of the school's English department, but the district administration didn't give her any choice. From the moment I entered the school, I had a target on my back. I wasn't allowed the luxury of getting to know the school or the curriculum, though I had not taught English Language Arts before; I wasn't even allowed to take some time to get to know the kids. An administrator observed my class the 5th day I was in the school. When I had a formal observation during my 3rd week, there were at least a half-dozen people watching me, most of them unknown to me. Then my principal was transferred to a district leadership position and a new principal took her place; she, too, came in to observe me.

When the new principal came into my room to talk about her observations, she asked me why I was there. I told her I had needed to get out of where I was, and this was the only position open I was qualified for. We talked a bit about middle schoolers, and I admitted they were my least favorite age group to work with. I said I thought I needed to go back to the Americans with Disabilities Act (ADA)/Equal Employment Opportunities (EEO) compliance officer and try to find another placement.

At the end of the day, the ADA/EEO officer called; I assumed the new principal had contacted her. She ordered me to go home until further notice. I cleaned my things out of the room and never returned. It was the end of January, 2010, and I had been in my new school for only four weeks.

The district never told me what they planned to do with me. A month later, I was called in to Human Resources to talk about my disability and possible accommodations. Nothing was said about my status with the district. I didn't know if they were going to continue paying me. I didn't know if I was eligible for unemployment benefits, since I didn't know if I was still employed. I didn't know what would happen to my medical insurance. I didn't know anything. The HR representative wasn't able to answer any of my questions.

A few days later, the accumulated loss and stress of the previous year and a half finally overwhelmed me, like a branch that breaks when the accumulation of snow becomes too much to bear. I made plans with a friend for him to come by in the morning. I left a note asking Keith to take Cody, Pepper, and Rascal. I gave instructions to return Grendel to the rescue agency I had gotten her from. I gathered together every pill I could find and washed them down with a tumbler full of vodka. I lay down on the sofa to sleep, forever.

I've never been so surprised in my life as when Cody woke me the next morning to go outside. I felt like an absolute failure. I couldn't even kill myself right. I posted something to that effect on social media, which led to a series of phone calls among those who read it, which led to Robyn coming over to check on me, with the police. They opted not to intervene because I wasn't a danger to myself anymore. The next day, Robyn took me to a psychiatric ER, who admitted me to their day program.

I attended the hospital program for about three weeks. I was broken, but still functional, and I had argued against the residential program given the four dogs I lived with. The program offered group sessions, individual therapy, and art therapy. Much of the information shared was practical how-to's on steps to take toward healing. I was comforted realizing that when it came to mental health—or the lack thereof—my problems were like everyone else's, but my reactions were not. I learned problem-solving solutions that I hadn't managed to pick up on my own. With the help of the hospital program, a psychiatrist, and a therapist, plus the support of friends and family, I slowly started to improve. The school district continued to pay my salary for the remainder of the school year. I began the hard work of rebuilding my life and looking for another job.

I was pretty sure my days as a public school teacher were over. I decided to try to find a position where I could apply my skills in a different setting. I had great computer skills, so maybe I could do clerical work. I was an English teacher, so maybe I could be a copyeditor or proofreader. Unfortunately, my job hunt started in March, 2010, at the tail end of the Great Recession. Suitable jobs were scarce, and not available to someone who was also changing fields. I could have cobbled together several part-time positions to equal a full-time position, but the pay would have been much less, and I couldn't have gotten health insurance; the Affordable Care Act had not yet made it possible for people in my situation to purchase insurance.

During the time I was looking for work, I was able to collect unemployment insurance. As that started to run out, I applied to be reinstated on disability. I started a small jewelry business, making and selling my own designs. The business failed, in large part because by the time I was able to figure out how to do what I wanted to do, I had no more money to invest. I knew I would soon be unable to pay my mortgage. I decided that if I didn't have a job by the end of 2011, I would start looking for ESL teaching positions abroad.

Robyn's marriage had ended in divorce in May, 2009, just a few months after the wedding and a month before I had moved to Baltimore. Pepper had died in June, 2010, at the age of 14, when her spinal arthritis advanced to the point she couldn't walk upstairs, jump up on the bed, or control her bladder. Keith's new partner had also passed away in the interim, and Keith had moved to Baltimore where he and Rascal shared a house with Robyn and Monkey. Grendel would have to go back to the agency that had placed her with me; I wasn't allowed to find another home for her under the terms of her adoption. That meant Cody would be going overseas with me. It was time for him to go back to school.

Once again, I went to the local Petsmart and registered Cody for a beginning obedience class. Six years earlier, he had benefitted from attending a class at a different Petsmart, but he hadn't actually learned anything. This time, I expected him to learn. The unanswered question was whether or not he could.

Cody seemed to enjoy our weekly trips to Petsmart. Once he learned where the classroom was, he would head in that direction as soon as we entered the store. In contrast to the other class, though, this time he was slower in walking from the front door to his class. He took the time to stop and sniff, though thankfully not to pee on anything. He greeted other dogs and people he met on his way. Once he was in class, he was reserved, but he wasn't frightened. He might sit under my chair, or he might not. His actions reflected his own mood and whims rather than his former perpetual state of uncertainty, anxiety, and fear. Cody was cooperative and willing to learn, especially because the lessons were positive and filled with treats and praise. There was one dog in Cody's class who was somewhat aggressive toward other dogs. Cody was unfazed by being a learning opportunity for that dog, even though it meant the other dog growled at him.

I told the teacher Cody and I would be heading abroad within the year. I was worried about the logistics of getting Cody wherever we were headed. He no longer used a crate, since he had destroyed all of his front teeth trying to get out of his crate years earlier. He remained especially fearful of men; it had taken six months for my friend Jude to be able to touch Cody without the dog flinching or backing away. Cody still had periods when he withdrew from the world because something frightened him, though those times were becoming fewer and less frequent. I seriously worried Cody would die of fright from a heart attack if he had to ride in a crate in a cargo hold, especially since men would likely be loading him. Loud noises were one thing that had always scared him. I knew how loud a plane ride was, and I couldn't even imagine how much louder a cargo hold would be. We agreed the best plan would be to call Cody my "service dog" so he could ride in the cabin with me. I'd probably have to tranquilize him, and he would likely still be frightened, but at least I could be certain he'd get there alive.

Cody's graduation portrait

I invited Keith to attend Cody's graduation from obedience class. It was a proud moment for both of us when Cody demonstrated what he had learned. There's an awkward picture of Cody with a mortarboard being held over his head by one of us while the other took the picture. To me, that snapshot is a symbol of how far Cody had come in six years. Now he would go even farther.

In 2012, it was remarkably easy to register a dog as a service dog. In the absence of a national testing and licensing standard, numerous web sites had sprung up which allowed people to get credentials for their pets by answering a few simple questions. They catered to people like me who, for whatever reason, wanted their dogs to travel with them, though some sites seemed more legitimate than others. Even though I was relieved it would be a relatively simple matter to call Cody my service dog, I resented that these bogus agencies existed. I was, after all, a special education teacher. I thought it was shameful these service dog scams could make money and allow people to subvert the laws that were put in place to help people with disabilities.

As I thought about the problem of fake service dogs, I was also anticipating the problems Cody and I might encounter in traveling. I realized he would need all the training of a service dog if I was ever to walk him through a busy airport. I found a wonderful book on training your own dog as a service animal. The first part of the book was the basic obedience Cody had already learned, but the second part included all the tasks a service dog might perform and how to teach them. One of the possibilities was for aiding balance. When I had been in China in 2008, I had fallen so frequently that it had become something of a joke among my colleagues. My sense of balance was bad enough I couldn't catch myself when I stumbled, and so I often fell, especially when getting out of the back seat of a taxi. I decided to train Cody as my balance dog, though I wasn't sure yet where we were going.

The only new command Cody had to learn was "brace," which meant to tighten his muscles while I placed my weight across his shoulders. This would allow me to pull myself up in the event of a fall. In theory, Cody would also brace to catch me if I started to fall, but I wouldn't know if he could do that until I actually stumbled, something that would be too dangerous for me to feign.

The other part of Cody's training was getting out in public to practice all his knowledge. I started to take him to my weekly therapy sessions. I bought him a "service dog in training" vest. While most handlers ask the public not to interact with or pet service dogs, I wanted Cody to learn that he didn't need to be frightened by new people. I had a patch put on his vest that said "ask to pet me." I also tried to carry around treats that strangers could give to him.

My therapy sessions took place on a hospital campus. We had to walk a block from the parking lot to the building, ride to the second floor on the elevator, and walk down the hallways from the main entrance to my therapist's office. The first obstacle Cody had to learn about was the elevator. I pressed the call button, and Cody and I waited, facing the doors. When the doors opened, Cody startled and tried to run away. The elevator was gone before I was able to get Cody inside, so we tried again. This time I was prepared for Cody's reaction and had hold of the handle on the back of his vest as well as his leash. I had to lift/drag Cody into the elevator. He crouched and trembled for the whole trip to the second floor. When we reached the second floor, he didn't want to exit the elevator, but I got us out before the doors closed again. Cody remained on a "down"—resting his elbows and stomach on the floor—for the whole 45-minute therapy session. He balked a little at getting back into the eleva-tor, but I was prepared for it now, and we made the trip down without incident.

The next week, Cody entered the elevator on his own, albeit in a crouch. He walked down the hall to the therapist's office with his head up. We had to wait in the hallway outside the office; over time, Cody became so good at staying down that often my therapist didn't notice him until she called us into the office.

Over the following weeks and months, Cody became an excellent service dog. As soon as I put his harness on him, his whole demeanor changed. He knew he was working, and he became steady and focused. He knew where to go and led me there. I experimented to see if he could guide me if I was blind-folded. It turned out that he could, even waiting for traffic to clear before crossing the street, but he didn't understand my position in space—as a result, he walked me into numerous door frames. Other than that, though, he did everything I asked of him and more.

He learned how to ride in an elevator. He learned to "sit" or "down" when we weren't moving and to sit at corners and cross-walks. He even learned the words "right" and "left," presumably because I spoke to him in a running narrative telling him where we were going; I certainly didn't intend to teach him directions. I started taking Cody out more places. However, I didn't take him to the grocery store—I couldn't imagine trying to manage him and a shopping cart at the same time, knowing that the cart itself would spook him.

The last thing I had to do to get Cody trained was get him a proper harness. Most commercial harnesses for service dogs had movable handles for the owner to grasp, but if I had tried to steady myself on a moving handle, I would have fallen. I went to a leather goods shop to get a custom-made harness with a fixed, rigid handle. It was comfortably padded for Cody, and it fit securely so that I could trust him to brace effectively. The handle put my weight across Cody's shoulders, since putting the weight on his back might have injured him.

We were ready to go; now all we had to do was get there.

Chapter 6

China

Avid Chip#089534829
Activedogs.com Registry #305344
Owner & Handler
Lauren Henry
Zibo, Shandong 255090
+86 5332851215

Cody's ID tag

THE JOB I accepted was in Zibo (*zee-bwa*), a 'medium-sized' city of 4,000,000 in the Chinese province of Shandong. My family, especially my three parents and Robyn, were supportive of me as I prepared for the move, but they were worried about my ability to survive in an environment so alien that I couldn't even read the street signs if I got lost. My reassurances that I had managed the environment without incident during my visit in 2008 didn't calm their fears. I was also going to be without a therapist for support after nearly 25 years of being in therapy. My suicide attempt had only been two and a half years earlier. Was my mental health strong enough to cope with the inevitable stresses of living in a foreign country? Keith had always managed our finances, and the fact that I was defaulting on my mortgage suggested to my family that I had not yet learned how to manage money. How was I going to deal with multiple accounts and bills both in the U.S. and in China?

I didn't know the answers to those questions, but I was willing to find out.

In order to travel from Baltimore to Zibo, we would first have to fly from Baltimore to a hub; next, we would fly to Beijing, where we would have to pass through Customs and Quarantine. I was worried about getting Cody through Quarantine. In theory, all dogs had to stay in the Quarantine section at the airport for a week and were allowed to remain on quarantine at home for a total of 30 days. There were suggestions all over the internet on how to travel with your service dog, but I had found nothing on the immigration process for a service dog or what documentation we might need beyond the health certificate required of all animals. I was in touch with an English-speaking vet's office in Beijing, and they were enormously helpful in guiding me through some of the paperwork both before I left Baltimore and after I arrived in Beijing.

Before leaving, I checked into the laws for service dogs in China. The concept was so new that in 2012, in all of China, there were only 40 guide dogs, and all of them served people with visual impairments. China's laws regarding service dogs' access to public places were similar to those in the U.S., but also new. I knew that many people would not yet have been asked to accommodate a service dog and handler. Cody and I were going to be teaching about service dogs and people with disabilities, whether we wanted the role or not.

Cody walked through the airport like the well-trained service dog he was. He ignored the noise and movement of all the people around him. He responded well to my voice commands and pressure from my holding his harness. I also had him on his leash; I told people who asked that the harness was for him to guide me, and the leash was for me to guide him. We really were a team.

Cody

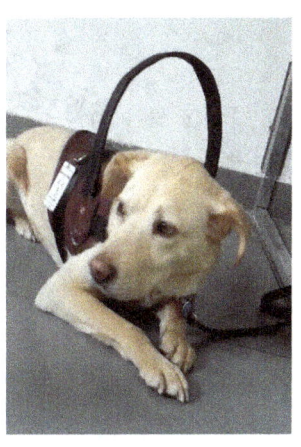

Cody in his working harness on a long down

For the first flight, we were near the back of the plane. Once on the plane, Cody sat at my feet, under the seats in front of us. He didn't quite fit, but our seat mates were understanding. Cody rested on a "down," and I thought maybe we'd get through this without too much upset. Then the plane's engines started, and Cody tried to exit the row from our spot at the window. My new seat mates helped me hold him back. I got him back on his down, but he was clearly upset. I had already given him his tranquilizer, but the vet had told me it was a low dose, and I could add to it if needed. I decided I would give him a second dose at the connecting airport; I just hoped Cody could hang on that long.

In the hub airport, I tried to find the area for Cody to relieve himself, but I was in worse shape than he was. I was tired, achy, and overwhelmed with all the movement and noise that was going on around me. I was worried about finding the dog relief area and getting back to the gate on time, especially since I hurt all over—mostly from fibromyalgia, but partly from stress. I asked one airport employee to help me, but his response was that it wasn't his job. I was starting to have a panic attack, something that usually only happened when I was driving and didn't know where I was going. I guess my face reflected my upset, because a couple stopped and asked me if anything was wrong. I told them that I didn't know where to take Cody and that I was in so much pain I wasn't sure if I could make it myself. Those kind people found someone, another airport employee, who called for a wheelchair for me. They even offered to walk Cody for me, but I knew he would be upset if a stranger walked him away from me. They waited with me until the chair showed up. Those two people were as close to guardian angels as anyone I've ever met. I hope somehow that lovely couple will read this, recognize themselves, and know how much their assistance meant to me.

Cody had never been exposed to a wheelchair before, since I'd never imagined a need to introduce him to one. He wasn't fazed by it at all. In fact, he pulled the wheelchair as he walked ahead and responded to my directions (left, right, keep going, stop). I was amazed, to say the least, since that was the first time Cody had demonstrated that knowledge. Visibly impressed, the attendant pushing the wheelchair asked me how Cody had learned all that.

I hadn't realized that Cody was a such a smart dog.

The next leg of our journey was a flight of about 13 hours to Beijing. I'll just say Cody did as well as could be expected. There were no major incidents, though neither of us slept. We went through Customs without any trouble, and all my paperwork was fine. We headed to Quarantine. I insisted that Cody could not stay in Quarantine; a service dog couldn't serve if he was locked up. In truth, I didn't expect to need Cody's help, but I was worried that the stress of our separation after the stress of flying might be more than Cody could handle. Also, every day that Cody was in Quarantine was a day I had to stay at a hotel in Beijing, a costly proposition.

It took a couple of hours, but eventually the woman in the Quarantine office allowed Cody to enter China. The holdup had been that I hadn't gotten a letter from my doctor verifying my need for Cody's services. It would have been easy enough to obtain such a letter, but it honestly had never occurred to me to request one. Cody would be on home quarantine for a month, during which he was not supposed to interact with other dogs. Luckily, no further paperwork was required.

The next day was the last leg of our journey: the train from Beijing to Zibo. The problems started the moment we entered the train station. The woman overseeing the X-ray and metal detector at the entrance didn't want Cody to walk through the screening device. We couldn't speak each other's languages, so in pantomime I asked if she wanted me to place him on the machine's belt. She shook her head no. I shrugged and shook my head, the universal pantomime for "I don't understand." Cody and I stepped aside while she searched for someone who could translate. While we waited, I contacted Emily, one of the assistants at the Beijing vet's office I had been in touch with.

The problem seemed to be that the people who dealt with the public didn't know that service dogs were allowed on trains. I handed my phone, with Emily on the line, to the supervisor who had appeared to take charge of the situation. When I again spoke to Emily, she confirmed my suspicions. The supervisor had to speak with someone higher up because she didn't know anything about the laws Emily had explained.

While they were trying to figure out what to do with me and Cody, the train I had planned to take departed the station. I made a quick call to my new school to tell them what was going on, so that no one would be waiting for me to arrive on a train I wasn't on. However, it didn't take long for Emily and the coordinator upstairs to confirm that Cody was allowed on the train. The supervisor escorted us to the next train and negotiated a seat change so that we were at the front of the car, which left a little more room for Cody. I got a quick picture of Cody, possibly the first service dog to ride on the train in China, as we settled into our seat and began what felt like the longest train ride ever.

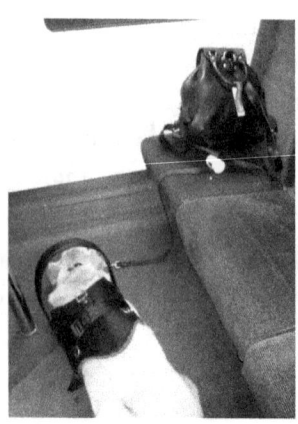

Cody waiting for the train to start

It wasn't that the amount of time we were on the train was onerous; I think it was only a couple of hours. However, Cody hated the train much more than the plane, and I hadn't sedated him enough. The sound was louder than the plane, and it came from all over. The rhythm of the wheels was anything but soothing to my frightened dog. Lying on the floor, Cody could feel every vibration. Additionally, the train was crowded, so Cody eventually ended up sitting between my knees instead of lying down at my feet. There wasn't an inch of spare room anywhere. I had to work hard at keeping Cody calm and focused during the trip. There wasn't any way for him to withdraw or hide; he had to simply cope until we could get off the train. Cody was an unhappy dog, which meant I was an unhappy dog mom.

The other passengers were curious about the dog and the foreigner who had suddenly appeared in their midst, but they couldn't ask me questions due to the language barrier. One brave woman sat next to me and asked in English why I had a dog if I could see. I told her about all the things dogs can do to help people, including helping with balance. I showed her Cody's harness and explained how he helped me. When we were done talking, some of the people standing around spoke with the woman. Although I couldn't understand the conversation, from the gestures I gathered that she was sharing what she had learned about me and Cody. That was the beginning of Cody's work as an unofficial canine goodwill ambassador in

China. There would be many such encounters over the next 33 months.

Gina, the young lady who picked us up at the train station, worked in the administrative office of the International Department. Gina's English was good enough for us to communicate well; in later months, I would notice tremendous improvement in her ability to speak and understand English as she spent more time working with the foreigners on staff. She escorted Cody and me to our new home—an apartment in a high-rise building. I was grateful for the height of the building because it meant that there was an elevator; Chinese buildings with fewer than eight floors were not required to have elevators, and thus few did.

My school paid for my apartment, like most schools in China that hire foreigners. Most schools also offered an allowance for utilities. All the apartment complexes I saw in Zibo had similar features. There was one main entrance to the complex with a security guard on duty at all times and fencing all around to prevent interlopers. Entrances varied from an archway to a retractable gate. Once inside the complex, several building entrances surrounded a courtyard or green area.

My apartment complex had two large buildings that faced each other across a large courtyard; each building had eight entrances. The apartments that could be accessed from one entrance couldn't be accessed from anywhere else. To get to my apartment, I had to walk through the main entrance passageway, turn right at the courtyard, and go to the fourth and last entrance. The ground sloped downward from the courtyard to the end of the building, with a retaining wall growing in height to the left of the sidewalk. There was parking inside each entry for the scooters and bicycles which many of my neighbors used for daily transportation.

My third-floor apartment had two bedrooms. The eating area was right at the front door; I ended up pushing the table against a wall and using it as an office space. The kitchen was small and U-shaped, just wide enough for one American cook— or two Chinese cooks. There was a 2-burner gas cooktop and a refrigerator. Chinese kitchens didn't have ovens or dishwashers; some had microwaves, but mine didn't. I eventually bought the biggest countertop oven I could find, which was large enough to roast two chickens or a small turkey.

The living room was large and bright, with windows that looked out onto the courtyard below. Just off the living room was a small room that filled the space between the wall of my bedroom and the windows. The primary purpose for this room was drying clothes, as there were two metal poles suspended from the ceiling. A pulley system allowed me to raise or lower one or both poles to hang up my wet clothes. When the poles were all the way up, even with clothes on them, there was plenty of room for storage or to make a little sitting area.

The bathroom was equipped with a Western-style toilet— no squatty potty here! Across from the toilet was the washing machine. Many Chinese washers have to be filled by hand, so it's helpful to have them near a water source like a shower. Chinese bathrooms typically have a shower space that's just a shower head coming out of the wall, similar to European show-ers. I was lucky to have an actual corner shower stall; it was big enough for me to take Cody in with me and give him a bath. The way the bathroom was set up, I could turn on the hot water and use the shower head like a garden hose to fill the washer so that I could wash clothes in something other than cold water.

Gina's job was to get me settled in; I would have dinner later that day with my new boss to get a sense of what I would be doing for the remainder of the semester. Gina's attentions included making sure I had at least minimal groceries until someone could take me shopping. In contrast, the university-owned apartment I had stayed in during my first trip to China, in 2008, had been bare. I hadn't even had a water machine (water cooler). For the first 24 hours I was there, I had had nothing to eat and had had to boil water in order to have anything to drink, so I was grateful that the school and Gina had thought ahead about my comfort.

My new job was teaching English in the International Department of a public high school. The International Department was a relatively small program of about 150 tuition-paying students within the larger school of around 4,000 students. Our students were 10th, 11th, and 12th grade students who hoped to attend universities in English-speaking countries. They received part of their instruction in Chinese from some of the same instructors who taught in the regular program, but the rest of their classes were taught in English by our department.

I can't speak with any authority about all schools in China, but I can share what this particular school was like, and I think what I saw was true for most Chinese high schools. For example, many of the students boarded at the school in dormitories, even if they lived in the area. Programming for non-residential students started at 8:00 in the morning and ran until 10:00 at night, Monday through Friday. There were eight class periods in the day, each running 45 minutes, and many classes met for a double period. There were breaks between class periods of 10 minutes each, including classes that ran for a double period. There was a morning break of 30 minutes between the second and third hours for students to exercise and have a snack. The lunch break lasted for two hours so that students (and teachers) could take a nap if desired; the dinner break was about an hour. The day ended with proctored study halls. Classes might meet two, three, four, or even five times per week, so the daily schedule varied.

In American schools, teachers generally have their own classrooms. While the architectural features and furnishings might be the same from one room to the next, each teacher has the opportunity to decorate their room in a way that reflects both the subject matter being taught and the teacher's personality. Teachers in China don't have their own classrooms; the students do. Students remain in the same room for all instruction unless special facilities are needed, such as a lab for science class or a studio for art. On Saturday mornings, in addition to interest groups and study sessions, the students had a period dedicated to cleaning their classroom.

The students remained in their group throughout the school day; I didn't see any evidence of electives or individualization. During the break between the second and third class periods, students assembled outside for morning exercises in all but the worst weather. The exercises allowed the students time to learn and display patriotism, similar to when American students recite the Pledge of Allegiance. There were also literal exercises; the students assembled in rank-and-file formation and jogged in unison around the campus once the loudspeaker instruction ended. Each group of students had one student calling out a chant, which reminded me of military drills.

Americans in general valued individuality, but in China the emphasis was on conformation. Americans said that "the squeaky wheel gets the grease," but in China, as in much of Asia, "the nail that sticks up gets hammered down." American teachers encouraged their students to think for themselves and ask questions, but Chinese teachers expected their students to sit quietly and absorb the knowledge which they, the teachers, imparted. Students had to memorize large amounts of information and recite or write it upon request. Chinese teachers discouraged questions because questions were interruptions and thus disrespectful. While many Chinese education agencies were collaborating with Western educators to expand their teaching to include more creative thought and less memorization, such initiatives had not reached Zibo in the time I was there.

Chinese students finished their formal high school studies at the end of 11th grade. The entire 12th grade year was spent preparing for the end of high school exam, the Gao Kao (*gow kow*, rhymes with how). A student's score on the Gao Kao determined what colleges they could attend, which in turn limited what majors they could have, and, therefore, what professions they could enter. However, our students did not have to take the Gao Kao because they didn't plan to attend Chinese colleges. Their 12th grade year was another full year of study, all in English.

Our program used the Global Assessment Certificate (GAC) curriculum, an Australian-based set of courses across several disciplines that prepared students worldwide for college-level study in English. When I first arrived at the school, students had to pass the GAC entrance exam in order to gain admission to the program. However, the exam was too difficult for many of the applicants. During the time I was there, the school changed to an open enrollment policy. We changed our programming to meet the needs of those students who wanted to study abroad but didn't yet have adequate English skills. After I had been at the school for about six months, I was promoted to a coordinator position and given the task of writing curriculum for an intensive 10th grade year of English studies for all students and a remedial program for 11th and 12th grade students who didn't meet minimum competency by the end of 10th grade.

Starting with the next school year, we administered the

GAC entrance exam to all the students at the end of the 10th grade, with three possible outcomes. Those students who could pass the entrance exam took the GAC curriculum for 11th and 12th grades. Students whose scores on the exam fell into a middle range took courses that paralleled a typical high school curriculum from a school district in Maine with which we coordinated; those students earned diplomas from both the Maine high school and the Chinese high school. The remaining students, who had scored too low on the exam to be in either of the other programs, took the remedial program I had designed for them

When I first arrived in October, 2012, the semester was already underway. I was assigned to assist another teacher in two Drama classes, since that area is one of my specialties. I had started studying acting at 8 years old, inspired by my mother's community theater involvement. I knew I didn't have the temperament to pursue acting as a career, nor, possibly, sufficient talent, but I enjoyed teaching and performing when opportunities arose. I had started to recognize that using acting exercises was a good activity for ESL students to practice their language skills in a fun, low-stress way. I was also assigned to teach a handwriting workshop—I almost choked on my meal when my boss informed me of this during our first dinner together. My handwriting had always been so notoriously illegible that when I told my dad about the workshop, he asked if I was doing it because no one else was available; my mother just laughed.

Although Chinese writing is precise, and students practice character formation from early in their studies, no one had ever taught the students the correct letter formation for the Roman alphabet. They were familiar with the idea of making strokes in the correct order for Chinese, so I demonstrated how to form the Roman letters stroke by stroke. Considering the complexity of

Chinese characters, I think my students found the lessons quite easy. At the end of the two-week workshop, I put together a penmanship contest, with prizes awarded by guest judges.

At the entrance to my apartment courtyard, there was a fountain, dry and filled with debris, surrounded by a low wall. On either side of the path from the entrance were large grassy areas. Each area had a round concrete table with curved benches. The seating, especially around the fountain, attracted people throughout the day. Children and their parents or grandparents tended to congregate between 4:00 and 7:00, when school was dismissed for the day but before dinner hour.

During the month of Cody's quarantine, I walked him in part of the courtyard away from other dogs. After a week or so, I let him explore that area without his leash. Once the quarantine period ended, and as Cody learned his way around, I started to let him explore a greater area off his leash. When he responded appropriately to my voice commands, he was allowed to be free; if he didn't respond as directed, I put him back on the leash immediately. The people around us probably didn't understand my English commands, but they could observe Cody's actions.

I learned quickly that Cody and I were the objects of intense curiosity and interest. People didn't know or care that he was my service dog; it was enough that I was a foreigner, and he was my dog. Most breeds that come from China are small, pampered dogs; the Chinese Crested, Pug, and Pekingese come to mind. Although at 60 pounds Cody was small for a Lab, he was much bigger than those breeds.

It seemed that everyone I met knew at least one English word: hello. I exchanged greetings and smiles with nearly everyone, especially the children. Their moms would encourage them to talk to me so that they could use the English they were learning at school. The typical dialog followed the formula taught in school.

"Hello!"

"Hello!"

"How are you?"

"I'm fine, thank you. And you?"

"I'm fine, thank you."

And then we would stare at each other while I smiled, encouraging them to continue, though they often looked confused or flustered. I would say something like "very good" or give them a thumbs up. Many ran back to their moms, proud of themselves for having spoken to the *laowai*, the slang term for anyone who wasn't Chinese. Some had more vocabulary and would ask more questions. The most common was, "How old are you?" In school, that question made sense; it was one of the first questions adults tended to ask children. However, in conversation with Western adults, it was not an appropriate question. In informal settings like the courtyard, I would just answer it; at school, I explained that it was considered rude.

For those who knew how to ask, what my neighbors wanted to know was what country I was from. The answer "America" always caused a lot of excitement; in early 21st century China, just as in Eastern Europe of the late 19th and early 20th centuries, America was the land of wealth and opportunity. Even more, America was the country they saw on TV shows and in movies. All Americans were beautiful and rich. Though no one ever said it, I wouldn't have been surprised to learn that they thought our streets were paved with gold. I did my best to represent my country well, since I knew I might be the only American my neighbors would ever get to talk to.

Cody started to become an extraordinary dog living in China. Some of it was a result of his training as a service dog.

He was responsive to every movement I made or command I gave. No matter where he was, if I called his name, he came immediately. I could even ask him questions which he answered by his movements. However, the change in Cody was more than simple obedience. Since I wasn't pulling on his leash, he was making decisions about what to approach and how. He could walk around things that frightened him, sniff them, or ignore them. He knew what he had to do—go to the courtyard or back to our building—and he did it. After the quarantine period ended, he played with the other dogs as much as he wanted while respecting the limits I imposed on how far away he could go. Cody was the only dog I'd ever had, other than Beowolf, who could have handled that degree of freedom. I was pleased that Cody had become so incredibly reliable; it was a function of his growing independence.

There were a couple of times when Cody got startled while we were outside. For example, Chinese often set off firecrackers for things like weddings and moving days. The loud noise was thought to scare off evil spirits that might harm the married couple or move into a new home to torment the residents. When Cody heard firecrackers, he would head straight for our entrance. I could never catch him, even if he was walking rather than running. In the early days, he tried to use any of the four entrances on our side of the building, and I was able to catch up to him to lead him to our entrance, with or without a leash. Eventually, he learned which door was ours.

One evening, as Cody and I were walking from the courtyard to our apartment, a man started up his motor scooter in front of us, blocking our way. The sound of an engine startled the dog, but instead of freezing and letting it pass by, Cody ran all the way back toward the courtyard with the scooter right behind him. He turned right to go to the courtyard while the scooter turned left to exit the complex. I couldn't see Cody in the dark, so I called his name. In a moment, he trotted all the way back to me with his tail waving happily; once the scary thing was gone, Cody was glad to walk back to our apartment.

When I had been in Zibo for about a month, my school asked me to participate in an outreach program with a rural school about an hour away. The administration figured that I was the logical choice because my teaching load was so light at that point. I may also have been the only teacher on staff who was certified to teach English in my home country. I was assigned to teach demonstration lessons to some of the students and introduce the Chinese English teachers to Western education methods. In order to do that, I was given an interpreter from my school plus a car and driver from the other school.

Gaoqing (*gow-ching*) Middle School No. 3 was located in a rural area. Despite the setting, the school had between three and four thousand secondary students drawn from several villages. It became obvious that many of the students in the school had never seen a foreigner in person before. I found their outright stares, complete with dropped jaws, to be a little unnerving. Still, I kept on smiling and greeting everyone, hoping that letting them see my warmth and humanity would show them more about Americans than my teaching would.

I had planned to teach greetings and social chit-chat using a drama game I called "Reception Line." First, the students and I brainstormed things you might say to someone at a wedding reception. Mostly, the list was greetings and common pleasantries. I told them they were all invited to my daughter's wedding. Half of the class would pretend to be my family members, while the other half were guests. I stood at the head of the family line, so I was the first person the 'guests' greeted. As the guests finished moving down the line, they joined the family side. As the last of the guests passed by, the first person in the family line joined the guests. Everyone had a chance to be both a guest and a family member.

I quickly learned that the students had no skills in listening and speaking. They were able to come up with phrases during the brainstorming, but couldn't figure out how to use those phrases in the role-playing game. I would later learn that Chinese English teachers focused their instruction on reading and writing, which was why native speakers of English were so highly prized as conversation teachers. Starting with the first lesson of the day, I kept adjusting the level down to meet my students where they were. In terms of speaking and listening, most of them were beginners.

At lunch the first day, the Headmaster and Assistant Headmaster of the school, as well as one of the English teachers, took Jenny, the interpreter, and me to a local restaurant. The hostess showed us to a private upstairs dining room. I had never attended a Chinese banquet before. The dining table was round, with a large, glass lazy Susan in the center. The place settings included a bowl with a small plate under it and a porcelain spoon in it. The deep spoon was shaped differently from a shallow Western spoon, looking more like the ones found in American Chinese restaurants. There was also a wrapped pair of chopsticks beside the plate.

I sat to the right of the Headmaster, who offered me wine. I refused, knowing I would have to teach later. Instead, I had a soft drink in my wineglass. Every time I took a sip, so did the Headmaster, often with a compliment or a toast. The other diners drank at the same time. I became so self-conscious I ended up quenching my thirst with tea instead, which is notable only because I don't like tea.

As the food rotated counterclockwise on the lazy Susan, the

Headmaster put things on my plate that he wanted me to try. At first, I rather resented his presumption, until I realized I was the guest of honor, and he was offering me the best from each dish. I experienced some new foods, including Chinese meatballs, sea cucumber soup, and some kind of fish. The fish had a tasty crust, but it was still fish, something I don't eat. The sea cucumbers were in a mild, tasty, slightly thick broth, but they had all the taste and texture of latex. The meatballs were okay, but the soup they were in was excellent. The only truly exotic food on the menu was donkey. Because of the communication barrier, I thought they told me it was "doggy," which I could never bring myself to eat. I just knew Cody would smell it on my breath—how could I ever explain it to him? I regret now that I didn't try the donkey dish, once I figured out what it was. It was a local delicacy, and unfortunately, I never got another chance to try it.

It was hard to be the guest of honor when I couldn't speak the language, even though I had two interpreters available. We talked a little about pedagogy—the art of teaching—and a little about Confucius, who was born nearby, but mostly I practiced the foreigner's smile, gazing into the distance at nothing while people carried on conversation around me.

After lunch, I had a question-and-answer session with the top students from each 8th and 9th grade class. There were about 150 students in the auditorium. Most of their questions were about my impressions of China or my personal likes and dislikes. I was surprised they weren't more curious about America, but perhaps they thought they knew everything from TV and movies. One girl asked if she could take a picture with me. I agreed, but had to refuse everyone else. When the session was over, another girl asked me to sign her notebook. I did, and suddenly every girl in the room decided to ask the same thing; the boys were too cool for that. I felt like a movie star being asked for autographs. It was unnerving being surrounded by so many people pushing things at me. I got a taste of why celebrities might not sign autographs all the time and why they have bodyguards.

The second day wasn't as long as the first. I brought my guitar and did fluffy lessons about animal names and sounds, followed by Old MacDonald and Bingo. However, for the one afternoon lesson, the men in the dark suits—headmasters and other local administrators—wanted me to teach the Chinese curriculum the way I would do it in the U.S., because visitors from all over the area would be coming in to observe. I gave them exactly what they asked for, from writing the objective on the board to creating an exit ticket to measure learning.

For the discussion with the visiting teachers afterward, I talked about the basic structure of an American lesson plan. The teachers didn't ask too many questions, though they may have been intimidated by the presence of the Director of Education from the provincial office. If you substitute State Superintendent of Education for the job title, that would be about the right level of awe. The first question was about testing in U.S. middle schools. I gave them a description of the No Child Left Behind legislation and the role testing played in federal funding. Blaming excessive testing on the government brought nods of understanding; I guess some issues, like teachers being told what to do by politicians, are universal. I hope I had something worthwhile to say; teaching kids was one thing, but being touted as an expert when you were just another teacher was a humbling experience.

My adventure in village teaching ran from Thursday to Wednesday. Over the weekend, I decided that I wasn't going to change anyone's life in a 40-minute lesson, so I decided to write a lesson plan that was little more than a fun review. It helped that I had been told I would never see a class more than once; I didn't have to worry about any follow-up. I pulled together a lot of pantomime, music, and drawing to get my meaning across. The students may have laughed at my stick-figure drawing of a cow, but at least they knew what it was.

On Monday afternoon, I took my show on the road to a nearby K-6 school. This one was even more rural than the first, like cows-and-chickens-in-the-street rural. We went to the principal's office first. There were several school officials, plus Jenny and me. They offered us plates of oranges, bananas, peanuts, and sunflower seeds, and passed around packs of cigarettes. I would later learn that fruits were always served whole, sunflower seeds were a favorite Chinese snack, and offering cigarettes was a sign of good manners and wealth, especially if they were an American brand. Cigarettes were also favors at the tables of the two weddings I attended while in China.

My lesson was with one class of 6th graders, while the rest of the grade observed. After the lesson, the elementary principal gave me a wonderful compliment. Speaking through Jenny, he told me that even though he didn't speak any English, he could easily understand my lesson through my voice and actions.

The men in the dark suits wanted us to stay for dinner—in my honor—but I told them I had to get home to let Cody out. My day was already two hours longer than usual because of the travel time. Instead, they invited Cody to attend school with me on Wednesday, my last day there, after which we were both invited to attend dinner.

Cody had not yet attended school with me because my school was reluctant to allow him on campus. When Jenny and I discussed Cody's attendance on the drive to school Wednesday morning, she suggested that maybe she could take him out of the room while I taught. I answered that we'd see how he did. Thus, I was adamant that Cody accompany me to class so we could see how he behaved. In the hallway outside the classroom, Jenny reached out her hand for the leash.

"No," I said, shaking my head.

"Cody does not go to the class," Jenny explained.

"I told you we would see how he did. We can't see if he doesn't go."

Jenny tried earnestly to explain the school's perspective, but I explained mine just as earnestly.

"Cody had to ride in the car for an hour. I can't leave him in a strange place with people he doesn't know. That's not fair." I almost had to stamp my feet and have a temper tantrum, but eventually Cody was allowed into the classroom for the first lesson. He lay down on the stage at the front of the room beside me and ignored the students. The only problem came when we sang Bingo. Remember that song, where you clap your hands in place of saying the letters? Clapping was one of the noises that scared Cody. Whenever the kids clapped, Cody stood up and paced. When they stopped, he'd settle down again. Other than that, he behaved perfectly. After the lesson, people started coming up to us and asking about him. I got to brag about Cody and, once again, teach a bit about service dogs and their training.

As it turned out, I didn't have any afternoon lessons, so the banquet was at lunch. I was disappointed to learn that the change in schedule meant that the elementary principal from the rural school would not be able to join us; after all, this banquet had been his idea. When it was time, the Headmaster, Jenny, a few teachers, and I all walked over to the dining hall together. As we chose our seats, Cody circled the table, choosing his spot. Eventually, he lay down under the table. The others asked questions about Cody throughout the meal. They wanted to know everything: details of his training, how he helped me, and what he ate.

I had heard that the school's chefs had won awards for their cuisine. For the luncheon banquet, they outdid themselves. They served us stir-fried cucumbers, roast duck, roast chicken, egg and green pepper, chicken and Chinese chives, breaded fried pork, pigs' feet, tofu with something green, fried peanuts, caramelized potatoes, and pork with peppers. In total there were 15 dishes and 2 soups for 7 people. The soups were meatball soup and egg-drop mushroom soup. Everything was delicious.

Towards the end of the meal, I noticed different people picking up scraps of food from their plates and holding them under the table. Cody was going wherever the food was being offered and taking bits of chicken, duck, egg, and pork from fingers and chopsticks. Cody was always delicate about taking food from hands or utensils. He used his lips rather than his teeth, and was so careful that the food would disappear from a hand without the person ever feeling the dog who was taking it. I think that gentleness was so unexpected that the others were intrigued by it. People fed him so much that I was afraid he'd get sick in the car, though luckily, he didn't.

Cody taught a lesson that day, too, about what a well-trained dog looks like and what he can do. The people who had been hesitant about allowing a dog into the school suddenly became huge fans. That would be the pattern throughout our time in China.

The end of my first month in China was marked by cold. Heat in China turned on and off according to the calendar, not the weather. In Shandong Province, the heat went on November 15, thus in early November it was chilly inside, no matter what it was like outside. I had had to pay for my heat in a lump sum up front, or presumably it wouldn't have been turned on at all. I was a little puzzled when Gina asked me if I wanted heat over the winter, but my colleagues soon explained the system. I also learned from colleagues that it was hot water heat, where pipes filled with hot water ran under the floor. Cody and I had different ways of dealing with the chill before the heat turned on; Cody took naps in the sunshine streaming through our living room windows while I added layers and blankets to keep myself cozy.

About the same time that my apartment started to warm up, Cody and I had an interesting experience in communication. We were in the courtyard when a woman came out with two adorable Bichons Frises. One dog stayed at her mama's heels, but the other ran ahead. I was sitting off to the side, checking email on my phone, so I got to watch the whole scene as big Cody loped over to sniff the adventurous little dog. Mama was horrified, thinking that the big dog meant to eat her baby. She grabbed the one close to her, then laughed as Cody and the other dog exchanged greetings, before the little one chased Cody away. Cody wandered off to sniff a bush, so I enticed the little dog over. I picked him up and handed him back to his mama, after which we were joined by an older couple and their grandson.

I saw the Bichons' mama was having a hard time holding both dogs, so I reached for the little boy dog again. The older man tried to ask me something, but I was still linguistically handicapped. However, he used pantomime, so I gathered that he was saying something along the lines of *you've come a long way*. I answered America, but that got blank stares. So, I said Meiguo, the Chinese name for America, which literally means "beautiful country"; in the local accent, it sounded like *may-gwa*. That registered, and the three adults talked about that for a bit before the conversation turned back to me. One of the few sentences I was confident about saying in Chinese was "I am a teacher," so I repeated that and pointed to my school, which was visible across the street. The man pointed to his wife and said she was a teacher, too. Of course, I didn't know enough

Mandarin to ask what she taught, and I probably wouldn't have understood the answer anyway.

Cody came up, so I let him sniff the dog I was holding, whom he'd already met. The little dog growled at Cody, who ran off again. We all laughed at the ferocious little beast I was holding, as well as the 60-pound chicken he had scared away. After a moment, Cody walked back to me and asked to go home. His communication was so clear that everyone else understood him, too. I told him okay, and said good-bye to the rest of the group, which in Chinese translates as "we see each other again."

One of my students had previously asked if I was lonely living in China. Oh, yes! There were people around me, lots of people, and I had friends at school, but those moments I had taken for granted in America—of sharing laughter with a stranger, joking with a friend, chatting in the elevator, or kibitzing when someone was trying to do something—those were mostly closed to me now. The thing that brought me the most pleasure, in a social sense, was when I smiled at someone on the street. There was that moment when they saw my face and recognized me as "other," then greeted me with a smile of their own. Not everyone did it, but I felt so welcomed and connected when they did. Laughing about dogs with other people fed my heart.

Although Cody was a trained service dog, my school wouldn't allow me to have him with me on campus. The sidewalks in China were usually made with paving stones or bricks rather than concrete. As the blocks shifted over time, the pavement became uneven. Most of the time I had no problems with that unevenness. However, I fell one Monday and again the next Friday, landing on the same knee both times, so when I went in to work to grade some exams that Saturday, I decided to take Cody with me. We hadn't even left the complex when Cody stumbled on a loose stone, pulling me off balance. Luckily, with him there to support me, I only stumbled a bit before I continued walking. How ironic would it have been if my balance dog had caused me to fall!

The few people who were at school that day were fine with Cody's presence; he lay down next to my desk and ignored them. I introduced people to him if they wanted to meet him, but mostly Cody remained uninterested in what was going on around him. Once again, the people at school got to see a well-trained, calm, and friendly dog. I hoped that the people who made the decisions would start to learn that a service dog was not the same thing as a pet, even though Cody was both.

A couple of weeks later, after some snow had accumulated, Cody got to demonstrate exactly how well-trained he was. For an officially atheistic nation, China had an oddly religious policy toward snow and snow removal: God put the snow there, God could take it away. Since nothing was ever cleared or salted, the snow would melt slightly during the day, and refreeze at night. We got a little more snow every two or three days that December, meaning that soon the sidewalks were covered in an inch or more of solid ice that no longer melted during the day. The roads were a bit clearer since the heat from the cars melted the snow and ice, but then again there were cars on the roads, so walking on them wasn't a safe option.

The school was fenced and gated on all sides. Even though I could see the school from the entrance to my apartment complex, I had to walk up the street to the corner, cross the street, walk down the block to the front entrance, then walk back in the direction of my apartment once I was inside the gates, just to get to the building which housed the International Department. The most recent snowstorms had left everything icy and dangerous. When I went to school another Saturday morning to work with some students, I harnessed Cody and took him with me. He kept me from falling three times by bracing, just as he'd been trained to do. The one time I did fall, Cody braced intermittently, slowing my fall so that I lowered to the ground gently and didn't get hurt. Then Cody, using the behaviors we'd practiced, carefully supported me so I could get back onto my feet. I gave him kisses and praise for being such a good service dog, and he earned extra treats that day.

The ice didn't melt away over the weekend, so Cody accompanied me to school again during the week. My boss and I conferred about how to make sure that I was safe walking to and from school while keeping Cody out of the classrooms. We agreed that Cody would remain in the office on a leash under Gina's control while I taught. My only concern was that Cody be safe, and I knew Gina would watch out for him. No one considered that Cody might have his own opinion.

When I returned to the office after my class, Gina was obviously upset, while Cody was lying down. Apparently, he had run out the door when he saw a chance, trailing his leash. Gina was right behind him, but four legs are faster than two, especially on ice. He went straight to the school entrance and turned right to walk down the sidewalk while Gina tried to catch him. He went to the corner, looked both ways, and crossed the six-lane road. He walked down the block to our apartment complex with Gina right behind him. He went to our entrance and walked up the stairs to our apartment. When Gina finally caught up with him, he was lying in front of our apartment door, waiting. She took his leash in hand and led him back to school. They had only just returned when I entered the office.

Gina already felt so bad about Cody's escape that I didn't need to say anything. Mostly, I was amused at how hard it had been to catch him, even dragging his leash, as well as impressed with his skills at finding his way home. My boss, who was an American, had to admit that they couldn't keep Cody safe at school, nor could I be safe walking to school without his help. I didn't use Cody's assistance every day from then on because I didn't always need it, but thereafter Cody was always welcome to accompany me to class.

Chapter 7

That's China!

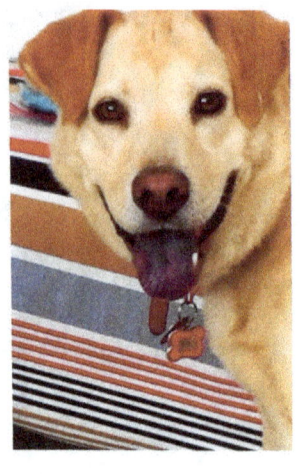

Cody was happy in China

Before moving to China, the only foreign country I had visited for any length of time was Italy. In Italy, it was considered an art form to cheat the system. People who accomplished it were lauded for being "furbo," which means sly or clever. Systems were designed with loopholes built in so that anyone who was clever enough could cheat.

In China, cheating was unthinkable, and systems were designed so that it was almost impossible to get away with anything. Thus, I had to pay for electricity in advance. I bought electricity from the apartment management, who credited the amount on a plastic card. I took the card to the meter, which was in a utility closet by the elevator on each floor. When I inserted the card into the meter, it credited me with whatever amount of electricity I had paid for. I had to repeat the process when I ran out of credit. I asked my colleagues how I would know when I needed to add more money to my card. They answered, quite seriously, "When the lights go out."

One evening, as I was cooking dinner, the lights went out. Fortunately, my gas burners were unaffected, so I was able to finish cooking. I spent the evening without power, during which I both lit a candle and cursed the darkness. The next day, I asked some colleagues to please explain a system where the signal to pay your electric bill was that the lights went out. They shrugged and said, "That's China."

I would learn over the years that the phrase "That's China!" was a useful mantra, repeated anytime a foreigner didn't understand the reasoning behind peculiar or contradictory behavior.

I used to refer to spring as "tushy" season. Everywhere I looked, in the courtyard, on the street, or while shopping, I saw little tushies. As soon as babies started to walk, they wore garments that had no seam in the crotch or seat. Instead, there was a slit that went all the way around, front and back. In spring, as the weather warmed, heavy coats were discarded, and the clothing underneath became visible. When the toddlers walked, you saw little tushies moving away from you. When they were seated in a shopping cart, well, you saw a bit more than that.

These peek-a-boo garments were toilet learning aids. When the child started to leak, the parent quickly put the child into a squatting position. This happened no matter where the child was or what the child was doing. And once the child was done "doing" it, the parent and child walked away with no clean up. Chinese pedestrians know to avoid random puddles, indoors or outdoors. As to the question of whether or not such customs are sanitary, the usual response from colleagues was "That's China!"

Most Chinese people don't view patents and copyrights the same way we do, leading to lots of infringements that we never see in America. For the most part, the Chinese believed that once something had been released to the public, whether it was a product or a book, it belonged to the collective community from then on. This attitude could cause our students a lot of problems once they were attending an English-speaking university, so we were careful to teach them about plagiarism. If they lifted words from a source without correctly attributing those ideas to the original author, they would have to rewrite their entire paper, if they didn't fail outright. One course assigned the students to write essays on plagiarism. Two students failed the assignment because their papers were plagiarized. That's China!

The management of my building turned off the elevator to the 2nd and 3rd floors. The reason, as I eventually learned, was that someone among the 2nd and 3rd floor tenants hadn't paid their elevator fee. However, I lived on the 3rd floor, and my landlord had paid the fee. It was hard for me to manage without the elevator, given my physical limitations, but the change was awful for Cody. We walked down three flights to go out, but when we came back, we took the elevator to the 4th floor and walked down one flight. Cody found it difficult to adapt to a new routine, and ran away from me twice in the time the elevator was turned off. The second time, he got spooked by new neighbors. I found him after 15 minutes of searching, in the stairwell on the 13th floor.

If someone had shut off a service in a dwelling in the U.S., the tenants would have pitched a fit. In China, no one said anything. The elevator was a battle I couldn't fight because of the language barrier, but no one else was fighting on my behalf. Chinese believe that the people in charge who make a decision must have a good reason for it and shouldn't be questioned. Even my boss's boss, who had lived in the UK for 5 years, couldn't bring herself to demand that they turn the elevator back on.

That's China!

Chapter 8

Spring and Summer

Cody looks excited to meet Kitty. Kitty looks unimpressed.

As WINTER STARTED TO THAW, Cody and I spent more time outside. The courtyard became a fun place to watch people who also watched me. I started to take walks around my neighborhood, venturing farther afield, sometimes with Cody and sometimes without. If I thought my walk might take me to places where Cody could be refused admittance, I didn't take him.

One Sunday morning, I put on my backpack and went for a walk alone. I knew there were fruit and vegetable vendors down the street, but I didn't know how far down. As it turned out, I strolled a total of only two miles, going down to the end of the shops and stalls and back home. Most of what interested me was outside, so I would be able to take Cody along in my future ramblings.

When Cody finally accompanied me on the same walk a few weeks later, he went on his leash, rather than in his harness.

He behaved so well that I allowed him to walk the last couple of blocks home without his leash. He was careful not to venture too far ahead of me, and I was impressed anew at how well Cody managed his independence.

Cody walking home from an outing off-leash. I call this picture "Independence."

The greatest fun about being out in the community was interacting with people, especially since we didn't share a common language. I did fine negotiating with vendors and storekeepers, even with my limited knowledge of Mandarin. Knowing American Sign Language was a big help, because it often indicated how to pantomime something. For example, when I was trying to find a vegetable peeler, I used the sign for "knife." The shopkeeper took me straight to the paring knives, and there was the peeler right next to it. I also got directions to the nearest ATM through pantomime, but alas! It didn't take my card.

Sometimes I felt I was a mobile museum exhibit. While I was browsing in one shop, a girl of about eight years old skipped into the store and waited impatiently while her mom entered the store behind her, all so she could say "hello" to me in English. She turned around and left immediately afterwards, dragging her confused mother with her. Other times, people would try to take my picture surreptitiously. I posed for pictures when asked, but I hated the photographic stalkers. I could just imagine them sharing my photo: "Look! It's Bigfoot!"

When people tried to talk to me, I shrugged and said "ting bu dong." People always laughed and repeated it when I said it. I started to wonder if it meant "I'm a stupid foreigner who is too lazy to learn your language. Laugh at me." Eventually, I learned that it was an idiom that meant "I hear, but I don't understand." I was never sure why my use of it caused laughter.

To help me on my outings and shopping trips, I bought a digital copy of a Chinese phrase book for my cell phone, as well as a translator app. When I wanted, say, a bottle of vinegar, I found the word in my book and showed it to the store owner. I never did find the word for zucchini; I thought I had bought one, but it turned out to be an English cucumber.

I also learned to take pictures of items I bought so that I could show store clerks what I was looking for the next time I needed it. When I went to the pharmacy the second time, I asked for everything I needed, none of which required prescriptions, by simply going to the counter and showing the clerk the photographs.

One of my favorite communications happened when I was out running errands and stopped at a McDonalds. The place was packed, as most places usually are in China. I finally found a little table, and sat down to eat. While I was nibbling my fries, a somewhat older gentleman asked if the other seat at my table was taken. I invited him to sit down. We talked for about 20 minutes or so. He was using broken English that he hadn't dusted off in a while, but it was still better than my Mandarin. He told me how much America interested Chinese people and how much they wanted to learn English. He talked about having learned from Chairman Mao that America was an imperialist nation, but that he could see now that we simply had ideas that were different. He thought it was good for China to learn from our ideas. I pointed out that it was also good for America to learn from China.

My unknown companion went on to talk about how well

President Obama spoke. He started chanting "Yes we can," and marveling at President Obama's ability to move an audience. He said another good speaker was Martin Luther King. He tied those two together, saying that King believed the color of someone's skin shouldn't matter, and Obama proved it. I enjoyed what he had to say, although he was difficult to understand at times. I gave him my email address and invited him to write to me, but I never heard from him again. It was those random encounters that made me love living in China.

A lovely landscaped area. My apartment building is in the background, in the center of the picture.

Spring has always been my favorite season. I loved watching the new leaves and blossoms appear. To me, there was so much hope and promise in every flower, just as there was in every newborn baby. I would watch day by day, seeing what new beauty sprang up in the world around me. There was a beautifully landscaped area that I sometimes chose to walk through on my way home. It didn't have any obvious reason for existing on an odd piece of land set back from two major roads. It was well-maintained, but it wasn't a park or play area—it existed solely for its own sake, a spot of natural beauty in an urban setting.

Each day on the way to and from school, I passed a row of small trees that lined the street. They were slower to get new leaves than the surrounding trees; by early May, some were still bare, with last season's brown leaves dangling from their branches and barely any green showing. When I had enough time, I would stop and talk to the trees. I would congratulate them on any new growth since the day before, then caress their branches and trunks. I would tell the slow ones that it was time to wake up and enjoy the spring. Often, I would sing to them; "Red, Red Robin" was a favorite. I was never certain what kind of trees they were, but the leaves looked a lot like bay leaves. I thought they might be laurels. I guessed they liked me because I was named after them—or maybe that was why I liked them.

Besides the flowers and the trees, as well as the aforementioned tushy season, a sign of spring was the start of the new semester after the break for the lunar New Year or Spring Festival. The Spring Festival moved around the solar calendar, but was usually in late January or early February. In addition to my regular teaching duties, that spring semester I was participating in a joint project between my school and a nearby middle school. The hope was to develop a feeder program for the middle school's best English students by exposing them to our foreign teachers. I visited six different classes in grades 6 and 7, seeing different grades on alternating Fridays. I knew in advance what curriculum the English teachers were teaching in their classes, which enabled me to design 40-minute lessons that coordinated with—and supplemented—those skills. One week, I taught the sixth graders about Easter celebrations. It was fun to see how excited the students got about all the kinds of candy that were in Easter baskets. The pictures of foil-wrapped candy spoke straight to the Chinese love of decoration, with a chocolate center.

Easter Sunday that year fell during the same week as the Tomb Sweeping holiday, where people went to the tombs of their ancestors, cleaned and decorated them, and left burnt offerings of food and money. They did this for two reasons: to show honor to their ancestors, and to keep the ancestors from haunting them. The Tomb Sweeping holiday probably has more in common with Halloween or Day of the Dead celebrations than Easter, even though the latter includes mention of an actual tomb.

A table at a Chinese BBQ restaurant

Another sign of spring in China was the appearance of barbecue restaurants in previously empty spaces. There was a vacant lot across the street from my apartment complex, in front of the fence that surrounded my school. One day, the space was no longer vacant. There were low, square, metal tables, surrounded by lower folding stools. At the back of this space, near the fence, was an area set up under an awning for cooking. These barbecue restaurants were little family-run enterprises, and the menu was pretty limited. There were skewers of meat, usually chicken, pork, and/or lamb. Granted, that was what the menu said, but when dealing with street food in China, all meat is mystery meat. There were also skewers of different vegetables, beef tendons, and thin, flat fish that caramelized as they cooked. The food was normally spicy, but it could be ordered "bu lada," or without spice. Customers also bought green onions and flat bread. The wait staff brought out a tabletop metal hibachi along with skewers of the raw or partially cooked food. The customers finished cooking the food over the hibachi, then wrapped the meat, scallions, and any sauce they wanted in the bread to eat it. I've never tasted anything like that kind of Chinese barbecue; it is one of the things I miss about China.

Once the restaurant had opened up right across the street from my apartment, I ate there several times with different groups of friends. One evening there were about eight of us, sitting around two tables that we had pushed together. I had Cody with me. The proprietor gave Cody a sidelong glance as we walked in, but didn't say anything. Then again, we learned after several beers that the men's restroom was a tree at the far end of the lot; the ladies' tree had a plywood board propped up against it as a privacy screen. The female members of our party took turns going to my apartment across the street for somewhat better facilities. Having a dog at our table was not the worst sanitation problem at that restaurant.

Cody was quite useful at our table. He happily cleaned up any dropped food, spills, leftovers, or scraps. When he wasn't scarfing down food, he was being his usual well-behaved self. People from other tables watched him, amused. Some brave souls, mostly children, came over to offer Cody bits of food. He almost always accepted them, gently taking the food with his lips or picking it up from the ground. Cody may have been wary of strangers, but he was still a dog.

Cody and I continued to enjoy the warm weather throughout the spring and summer. While it was sometimes uncomfortable during the daylight hours, the evenings were pleasant. One evening we were outside at around 6:30, when all the toddlers and their moms were outside. Cody didn't like the toddlers when they were on the ground, but he sniffed their feet when their moms were holding them. There were also about five other dogs outside, along with their humans. Everyone knew Cody's name; they tried to call him over, but my skittish dog didn't approach strangers. Then Cody shocked me; he walked over to one woman who was sitting down, holding a poodle. He stood there calmly while she patted his head. I stared in disbelief. Cody? Seeking petting from a total stranger? Without treats to bribe him or anything? The dog's dad tried to pet Cody, but he ducked his head away from the oncoming hand and walked away.

Ah! There was the Cody I knew. I tried not to giggle.

When school closed for the summer break, many of the foreign teachers went home or on holiday. Cody and I ended up with a houseguest for the summer. He was a white cat with a grey smudge on his head. His name was JD, but he preferred to be called Kitty. The first time Cody and Kitty met, we got a cute picture of the two of them sharing a sofa cushion; Danielle, Kitty's mom, and I were sure the two of them would be friends. A couple of weeks later, Kitty moved in to stay while his mom went home to America. We didn't see Kitty again for a couple of days. He started to come out every evening at around ten, when he got a meal of wet cat food. Cody was concerned about his new friend. Every time Kitty made a sound, Cody would come running from wherever he was in the apartment. I joked that Cody was starting to believe his name was "Meow."

On the 4th of July, I hosted a cookout for some school friends. There were seven of us; a mix of Chinese, American, Canadian, and British, sitting at one of the outdoor tables in the courtyard. I had bought a little grill at one of the shops and found charcoal to burn in it. I made hamburgers, hamburger buns, baked beans, and potato salad. Others brought pulled pork, spaghetti, chicken wings, and a bunch of other stuff. Everyone brought what they wanted to drink: beer, Jack Daniels, wine coolers, and soft drinks. We even had a homemade pecan pie for dessert. The only thing we didn't have was fireworks, despite an all-out effort by the resident pyromaniac to track some down. We thought surely we'd be able to find fireworks in China, but we were wrong. Fireworks were only for sale around the Spring Festival. Nonetheless, we had a great time, even without Cody. He had remained in our apartment in deference to a guest who was afraid of big dogs.

One of the attendees was an American teacher who would be starting work at my school when the new term started. Jon had just moved to Zibo from Wuhan. With him was an adorable little toy poodle named Xiao-Xiao, which means "little, little." Xiao-Xiao was in a carrier slung over Jon's shoulder. Jon had been sitting on a bench in Wuhan when this little brown dog came up to him.* The dog was a mess, undernourished, and begging for food. Jon took him home, fed him, and cleaned him up, only to find to his great surprise that the little dog was actually white. Jon figured that the dog had to have been on his own for a long while to have gotten that underweight and that dirty, so he decided to keep the dog, and his students had suggested the name Xiao-Xiao. I told Jon we should get our dogs together to play.

Xiao-Xiao/Shadow

When Cody and Xiao-Xiao met about a month later, it didn't happen the way Jon and I had hoped. Jon had a health emergency and had to be evacuated back to the U.S. Xiao-Xiao couldn't travel with him on such short notice. Our boss asked me if I would take care of the little dog

---

* Until the Covid-19 pandemic, no one had ever heard of the town where Xiao-Xiao/Shadow had been rescued.

until Jon could make arrangements to ship him. Of course, I said yes.

The dogs got along, though Cody was a bit jealous at the appearance of a rival for my attention. Kitty disappeared again after Xiao-Xiao arrived. I knew Kitty was still alive and well in the apartment somewhere because the food dish was empty, and the litter box was full. He came out of hiding after about a week. By then, Xiao-Xiao had accepted Cody and me as his pack.

Kitty delighted in torturing Xiao-Xiao, especially by sitting on top of the TV and teasing the little dog. If Xiao-Xiao got too close, Kitty would cry. Whenever Kitty cried, Cody went over to make sure his kitty was okay and scold Xiao-Xiao with a soft growl. Then, Cody and Kitty would exchange head sniffs, and Cody would walk away. Xiao-Xiao was jealous because he wanted to sniff Kitty, too. So, I would call Xiao-Xiao to me, and he would jump up beside me for a tummy rub, prompting a jealous Cody to stick his head between Xiao-Xiao and me. One night I was trying to pet both dogs while comforting the cat, and ended up speaking in Seussian rhyme:

I live in a zoo. I do! I do!

I live in a zoo, with you, you, and you!

And I wouldn't have wanted it any other way.

I wasn't sure how long Jon had had Xiao-Xiao, but the little dog's fur was long and matted, so my friend Xuan "Sally" Li and I took Xiao-Xiao in for grooming. I had thought he was just going to get a trim, but he had had so many knots and mats in his fur that they had had to shave him. I didn't even recognize him when I picked him up. As Sally and I were heading back to my apartment, I was carrying Xiao-Xiao in his shoulder bag carrier and didn't see a small step; I stubbed my toe on the step and fell.

I had tried to protect Xiao-Xiao from injury, but had ended up injuring myself, landing on my knees and elbows. It didn't seem to be a serious injury for all that it hurt at the moment.

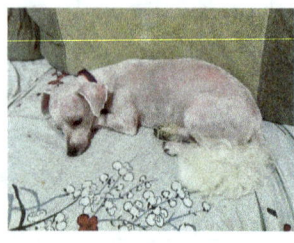

A subdued and hairless Xiao-Xiao/Shadow

When we got back to my apartment, Cody wasn't fooled by Xiao-Xiao's appearance, but Kitty seemed to think I had brought home yet another dog. Xiao-Xiao was so traumatized by the shaving that he spent the rest of the day and night cuddled up beside me— poor naked little baby!

The new school year started a couple of days after Xiao-Xiao's grooming. Getting up early again for the first day back at school, we saw Cody's favorite playmate in the courtyard. Momo was a cocker spaniel who was about halfway between Cody and Xiao-Xiao in size and weight. It was like having a 4-year-old and an 8-year-old on a play date with a 6-year-old. Both my boys were excited to see Momo, and both could play with him. When the two bigger dogs were playing, though, they almost bowled over poor little Xiao-Xiao. I was pleased with myself because I was able to tell Momo's mom in Chinese that Xiao-Xiao wasn't my dog and that he was naughty.

Since I was a coordinator, I had a part to play in the teacher training during the induction week. Being on my feet again, the injuries I had suffered when I fell started to be a problem. A few places had hurt right away, like the toe I had tripped on, and my knees and elbows, which I had landed on. It wasn't until sometime on Monday, two days after the fall, that I noticed an aching pain in the arch of my right foot. I hobbled around for the next couple of days, teaching my workshops as planned, taking ibuprofen, and putting Cody to work in harness to keep me from falling again. I finally had to ask for help going to a doctor and ended up having my first experience with health care in China.

Stephanie, the current person assigned to assist the foreign teachers—a.k.a. "the new Gina"—took me to the main hospital. She bought me a plastic card for the hospital which cost 10 ¥, or less than $2. We went upstairs to a clinic. One of the security guards was tickled at the idea of helping us and made himself our personal escort, even though we didn't need one. He carried my backpack around, and chased people out of chairs so I could sit. I had gotten used to the special treatment foreigners often got because we were considered unusual, but his attentions verged on embarrassing. However, he was so proud of being part of whatever was going on and answering questions from curious passersby that neither Stephanie nor I wanted to shoo him away and disappoint him.

The exam took place in an open room, with the doctor seated on one side of a small table and me seated beside him. Stephanie, the guard, and the next patients in line were all standing around; health care privacy is a concept that didn't seem to exist in China. The doctor poked at my foot a few times, wiggled it, made me scream in pain, and diagnosed a strained ligament. He wrote out a prescription, and we went down to the pharmacy.

Stephanie took my card, along with $50 and the prescription, to the cashier, who put the money on my card. Then Stephanie went to the pharmacy, which dispensed 2 boxes each of 3 kinds of medicine. When I had a chance to search the English names online, I found they were herbal medications, including a bandage that I had to apply which had a Tibetan herbal medication saturating the pad. Sally came over later and read the boxes for me. She told me that one was specifically for pain from foot and ankle injuries. Another was also for pain, but somehow different. Frankly, I didn't care what the medications were, as long as they worked.

I don't think we were there longer than an hour. I didn't have to get x-rays since the foot was obviously not broken. Even though I still had to be on my feet, the injury seemed to heal faster than it would have without care. My initial assessment of Chinese health care was generally positive. I was pleasantly surprised.

Unfortunately, this impression wouldn't last.

One of my last duties before leaving the high school at the end of my contract was to observe the teachers in my program and make sure they were implementing the new curriculum correctly. One of my teachers was working with a group of students from the new tenth grade class, whom I'd never met, so she introduced me as "Lauren Teacher." When I got home, my neighbors encouraged their young children to tell me "Laoshi, ni hao," which means "Hello, Teacher."

I was both amused and puzzled—when had "Teacher" become part of my name?

Chapter 9

New School

Xiao Xiao/Shadow

My school did not offer me a contract for a second year, so I spent much of September searching for a new job. Danielle, Kitty's mom, gave my name to her boss, who hired me to work at a different school operated by the same agency. Since my school had paid for my apartment, taking a new job meant moving to a new apartment. I would still be in Zibo, but I would be in a different part of the city. My new school was in an industrial park area at the outskirts of town. It was much too far to walk or even bike, so I was going to have to take the bus to get to and from work. Luckily, I found a nice two-bedroom apartment a block from a bus stop. The new school's van and driver helped move me, along with everything I had acquired over the year, plus the two dogs. I moved after the "Golden

Week" at the beginning of October, when everything shut down for the Chinese equivalent of Independence Day.

At about the same time, Jon discovered that flying Xiao-Xiao to the U.S. as unaccompanied cargo would cost about $2000. Since he couldn't afford to pay that, Jon thanked me for taking care of Xiao-Xiao, and told me he would try to find an adoptive home for him. I knew Cody would miss having his friend around, so I offered to adopt the little beast. I wasn't sure if Cody was getting a little brother or a little bother, but at least he'd have a playmate.

My new school was a boarding school for grades 1-8. Yet again, the administration asked me not to take Cody to school with me unless it was essential. I was assigned to teach all five of the first-grade classes, a total of 150 students. My lessons were 30 minutes long, Monday through Friday, but my schedule was different every day. Unlike most of the foreign teachers in Zibo —and probably in much of China—I was equally qualified to teach in China or America, so the supervisor told me during my interview that he wanted my lessons to look as much as possible like the lessons that I would teach in an American classroom. However, three semesters later, he would dismiss me for not teaching like everyone else. That's China!

My new apartment was a little smaller than the old one, but also a little nicer, though both had the same number of rooms. The space for hanging up laundry was in the larger bedroom, creating a small nook for a desk and computer. The bathroom was smaller than the old one, with the clothes washer next to the sink, which was next to the toilet, which was next to a shower area. I was sad to lose my shower stall and the ability to wash my clothes with warm water, but otherwise I liked the new apartment.

One oddity about the new apartment was the arrangement in the kitchen. There was one counter in the galley kitchen, with the cooktop and sink in line with the counter. At the far-left end of the counter was the refrigerator. Its handle was on the left side of the door, so the door opened out into the room. The refrigerator plus the open door were almost as wide as the kitchen was deep; there were only about two inches of clearance between the edge of the door and the wall when the door was opened. There was no way an average sized adult could reach around or over the door and into the refrigerator when it was open.

I knew that it was a relatively easy matter for an appliance store to move the handle to the right side of the door and hang it so it opened the other way, but I had no idea how to make that happen in China nor even how to describe it in Chinese. I ended up moving the fridge into the living room. Few people commented on seeing a fridge in a living room, but for those who noticed, the position of the refrigerator door handle was another "That's China" moment.

Keeping that fridge full by grocery shopping became one of my favorite activities while I lived in China. Those weekly trips were like mini tests of how well I was doing at adapting to my surroundings. I could still get an awful lot accomplished with point-and-grunt communication, but I kept picking up new words and learning to combine them with ones I already knew.

Most of the time I went to the grocery store at one of the local shopping malls; I could pronounce the name of the mall, so getting there by taxi was easy. However, as I learned the bus routes, I discovered that I could get to the shopping mall where the local Walmart was by simply staying on the bus an extra stop past my regular stop on the way home. There was another mall with a grocery store, but that one was a little harder to get to, even on the bus.

I kept a list in my head of the different items available at each store. When I put together my weekly shopping list, I chose which store to visit according to what was on the list. I had a photo album on my phone of grocery items I used so that I could ask for things without necessarily knowing their name in Chinese.

Meat was particularly difficult to shop for. It wasn't sold in sanitary packages with price stickers on the label. It wasn't even sold behind glass encased counters. Meat was displayed in open bins, where customers examined it with hooks, tongs, or scoops. The meat cutter would cut or trim the meat according to the customer's directions, put it in a bag, weigh it, and sell it. The cuts of meat weren't what we're used to in the West. Fortunately for me, my grandfather was a kosher butcher, and he had taught my mother, who in turn had taught me. I could recognize a shoulder, rump, rib, or loin even when there wasn't a sign—well, okay, there was a sign, but it was in Chinese. I developed a good relationship with one of the meat cutters at my usual store. She was able to understand my gestures and pantomime, and I understood her when she explained something about the meat on display. When she saw me, she would point out cuts she thought I would like or that were on sale.

The foreigners in town were excited when a new grocery store opened. Of course, we were also excited when a new Burger King opened. Excitement is a relative term for expats in China. The new grocery store was part of a European chain and was reputed to have a great selection of foreign foods. A friend and I went to check it out, but there were a lot of things we didn't buy on that first trip because we weren't sure how to get them home; there was a limit to how much you could carry when you were dependent on taxis for transportation.

The new store was amazing. It carried a wide selection of products that seemed to cater to foreigners, though there weren't that many of us in the whole city. They stocked good cheese in a wide variety: feta, Greek sheep's milk cheese, and Greek goat's milk cheese. I didn't even know there were differences among them. They had Philadelphia™ cream cheese, just right there in the cooler, waiting to be bought by us mere mortals. I was in cheese heaven.

The meat was cut into familiar shapes in packages with both English and Chinese labels. I found a boneless rib roast for sale; I could buy one and slice it into steaks. Maybe I would get a rump roast, for roast beef, or a chuck roast, for pot roast. Having things labeled so I could read them really widened my menu options.

I found herbs and spices I hadn't been able to buy locally, though I had arrived in China with lots of herbs and spices in my suitcase. I found fresh dill in the produce section and dried oregano, bay leaves, and fennel seed along with other herbs and seasonings. In the alcohol department, I found an Italian sangiovese table wine that looked like it was decent. I even found amaretto, something I had been trying to find for months. The prices weren't all that bad, but the packaging was like that found at a buyer's club, so I bought more than enough of some things to last for the rest of my time in China, and spent more money than I had ever spent in one shopping trip. There were a few things on my "foods I miss" list that I didn't see, but the store was constantly being restocked with new items.

When I returned to the store the following month, one area had been remodeled, which meant the shelves throughout the store had been rearranged. I couldn't find the pet aisle, and I had to plan out how to ask for dog food. I used "I want" in Chinese, followed by the sign for "eat/food" and a picture of Cody on my phone. I figured I'd either be shown the dog food or fresh dog meat. I was so glad they didn't take me to the meat case.

As I got to know more foreign teachers in Zibo, I started to think that going to China to teach English was a lot like joining the French Foreign Legion—or the Klatchian Foreign Legion, if you prefer. The requirements were minimal: a university degree in anything, plus some kind of credential in Teaching English as a Foreign Language (TEFL). Not everyone had even the minimum; I knew foreign teachers with a degree, but no TEFL training, and foreign teachers with a TEFL certificate, but no degree. Rules in China were flexible, especially if a school had the connections to offer a well-placed bribe. Functionally, almost anyone could join our ranks.

Once you arrived in China, you left your past behind. No one knew who you were, where you came from, or what you had done in the past, nor did you know anything about those closest to you. Like serving in an army, you formed relationships with people you might never have spoken to in your old life. The relationships were just as deep and precious as any you had experienced before, but in the back of your mind, you wondered what the folks back home would think of the company you kept.

Since no one knew you, you were judged only by what you did while you were there. You got the chance to find out who you were when no one was watching. I learned a lot about myself; I wasn't who I thought I was. I was actually a kinder person than I had given myself credit for being. On the other hand, I got to see the ugly side of other foreigners. There were people who wanted the adventure of teaching in China, but who had no respect for the Chinese people or their culture.

Most Chinese students studying English had an English name. I had always been ambivalent about that practice. When I had taught beginning Italian at Florida State as a graduate assistant, I hadn't given my students Italian names, but I had pronounced their English names as I would have pronounced them in Italian. There was something to be said for having a name that was easily said in the target language so that it didn't disrupt the flow of speech. I believed, though, that names were so integral to identity that it was unfair to change someone's name for one class a day. The opposite argument was that using a different name drove home the point that, while Shen Feng Yi might speak Chinese, Molly Shen spoke English. The name theoretically would also trigger use of the foreign language, which is stored in a different part of the brain than the native language. I'm not sure if there was research to back those theories up, but it sounded good to parents.

I didn't have a choice at my new school; the kids were given English names by my predecessor, who had apparently been something of a jerk. He had treated the process of naming the kids like it was a joke and gave them truly awful names. In one class alone, I had a Gene, Gina, Jen, Jenny, and Jin, not to mention having both Sean and Shawn in a couple of classes. I wondered why on earth he'd made it hard on the students and teachers by giving the kids names that were hard to distinguish from each other. I also had Aristotle, Ghandi, and Jesus—in English, not Spanish—as well as Future, Turbo, Nintendo, G, DaVinci, Yoko Ono, and Charlie Brown. Spiderman, Dr. Seuss, and Yukon also made an appearance on my rosters. Some of the kids had Spanish names like Juan, Luis, and Ernesto; imagine trying to explain the pronunciation and spelling of a Spanish name to a Chinese student in an English class.

While I might not have particularly cared for the practice of giving the kids English names, I did think that if we were going to do it, we should do it responsibly. I spent a few hours researching and collating the most popular baby names for the US, UK, Australia, and Canada from 2010, the most recent lists available at the time.

Comparing the data for the four countries was interesting. Some trends seemed universal. For example, female names ending with 'e' were giving way to names ending with 'a'. Thus, Anna, Diana, Maria, and Olivia were on the lists, but Anne, Diane, Marie, and Olive were nowhere to be found. A lot of names were on both the boys' and girls' lists, even Charlie, which surprised me. Although the name "Cody" was listed, I didn't give that name to any of the students; there was only one Cody in my life.

When I was ready to give my students new names, I did a little ceremony that had more in common with a Brownie Girl Scout initiation than a christening. Some of the students were nervous about what their new names would be, but in the end, they were all happy with their new names, even the ones whose names I didn't change.

A couple of weeks later, one of the Chinese English teachers thanked me for the name changes. She said that the children changed names every year, but now that they had "nice" names, maybe they wouldn't have to. She also explained that the parents had called the Chinese teachers to complain about the awful names, but the Chinese teachers had had nothing to do with the process, since the foreign teachers always did the naming. I doubted the foreign teachers had ever heard the complaints, since there was no real communication between the two groups.

This teacher paid me a sweet compliment: she asked me to find a good English name for her. She had chosen the name "Feeling," but later learned it wasn't a real name. I suggested "Felicity," "Felicia," or "Felice," since they all came from the Latin word *felix*, meaning "happy," which is the same origin as "feeling." She chose Felicia.

Similarly, I wanted to change Xiao-Xiao's name to some-thing English, since he would eventually be an American dog.

His name sounded like the first syllable in "shower." I ended up naming him "Shadow," which was phonetically similar to Xiao-Xiao. I got teased a bit for naming a white dog "Shadow," but I liked the suggestion that I should adopt a little black dog and name him "Ghost" to make a complete set.

I was hit with a bad case of laryngitis during my first week at the new school, which was especially difficult given that my lessons were essentially 30 minutes of singing, five times a day. I recovered after about two weeks, except for an occasional squeak, by which time I had learned just what kind of situation I had landed in. There were five foreign teachers in my school; I was the only female. Among us, we had one teacher each from the U.S., U.K., Australia, Canada, and Cameroon.

The school didn't have a curriculum, just an assortment of suggested materials. There were no objectives or goals, scope and sequence, or any of those things that professional teachers would expect to find already in place. Without a curriculum to offer guidance, I started my new job by writing a complete foreign language curriculum for the first grade, which was their first year of studying English. Then I started implementing what I had written.

The best part of my new job was my students; they loved me, and I loved them. When I walked down the hall or into the cafeteria, I was greeted by a chorus of hellos, and not just from my own students. If my students were nearby, I was likely to end up being mobbed with hugs or high fives. The worst part of the job was that I couldn't chat easily with my kids. I was doing well learning new words or phrases, but I had a limited vocabulary and a lot of trouble understanding when people spoke to me. I sometimes sat with my students at lunch and wished I could understand what they were chattering to me about.

It was important to me that my students got lots of praise and affection from me. Although each class had an assistant who took care of the children in their dorms and attended their classes, I knew the assistants wouldn't have much time to pay attention to each student. My heart went out to these youngsters, who lived most of the time at a boarding school without their parents or someone else to love them. I wanted to help fill that gap.

My other concern was that classroom discipline in China was quite different from the U.S. Humiliation, shame, yelling, and physical punishment were all permitted and widely practiced. I once saw a teacher at the high school yell at a student in Chinese until he finally started crying. She told me later that crying was her goal; she had intended to continue yelling as long as it took to make him cry. I'm not sure what she said that made a teenage boy cry in public, nor why she considered that a good practice.

I had seen the assistants in my five classes do things like slap a child's head, grab them by the arm to throw them to another place (into the hall or the cloak room), kick them, or whack them with a yardstick. I watched an assistant shatter a long plastic tube when she slammed it on a desk as she scolded the students. I was horrified, but I wasn't in control of the situation; I was just a witness while I was unpacking before a lesson or packing up afterwards. Reporting those incidents to my supervisors hadn't changed anything. I decided the best thing I could do was to model other ways of shaping behavior, as well as letting the kids know that I valued them as individuals no matter what kind of students they were.

I loved what I was doing. I had never had a job that offered as much variety and fun as I was having. I drew on nearly everything I had ever learned or experienced in designing lessons for my classes; my knowledge of sign language, drama, music, art, education theory, and foreign languages all informed my teaching. I prepared one lesson a day and taught it five times to adorable first graders. Each lesson was almost all music and movement. I introduced English vocabulary and phrases that the children already understood in Chinese. For example, I might introduce English color words, but my students already understood color concepts. In fact, I specified in the curriculum I wrote that the English language content must always be lower than the students' instructional level in Chinese, to make sure that the English classes were all about the language, not the content.

I put together a slide show nearly every day which functioned as my lesson plan. We did hello and goodbye songs, the calendar, some new information, and lots of songs and rhymes. "Little Bunny Foo-Foo" was a favorite, though I was pretty sure they didn't get the "Little Goony Foo-Foo" punchline. The image I used in my slide show for the Goony Foo-Foo was from the Bugs Bunny cartoon where he took the Jekyll/Hyde serum; I had way too much fun searching for exactly the right graphic images.

I tried to recognize and learn the needs of my students, as a whole and as individuals, so that I could teach in a way that met those needs. In every teaching job I've ever had, there has always been a student who was extra special. That was part of my reason for going into special education in the first place— to find and help those students who needed a little extra. Often their specialness was a unique way of thinking and learning, so my job became finding a way to cultivate their specialness so that they could become the best version of themselves.

Megan was such a student.

Megan

Her teachers described her as "naughty." She wiggled all the time, picked up anything within reach to examine it, talked out in class, and, though I couldn't understand what she said, I suspected she was a bit of a smart ass. She was frequently being punished for her misbehavior when I worked with her class, though I never saw what she had done since it always happened before I entered the room.

Because of her behavior, her desk was right next to the teaching station. I could hear everything she said during my lessons, including those things she muttered under her breath in English. Those whispered utterances showed me how much more she was learning than even her brightest classmates. The irony was that I would never have heard her had she not been sitting so close as a punishment for misbehavior.

I realized that Megan was leaps and bounds ahead of her classmates, at least in English. She remembered everything from all our previous lessons and was able to apply what she learned in new situations. I suspected that her 'naughty' behavior simply came from being a gifted child who was bored. She was also a nonconformist growing up in a conformist society.

I got permission from my boss to start working with Megan one-on-one during the long lunch break. I talked to her teachers, who loved the idea. Right after I talked with the teachers, Megan's mother showed up to take her home from the boarding school for the weekend. I got to talk with her mother, too, through an interpreter, and I think she was pleased that Megan was getting some special attention, especially since I refused any payment for the tutoring.

I started teaching Megan to read, using the same methods I had used tutoring young ESL students in America. We started meeting twice a week, though I quickly realized I might have to change to three or four times a week to keep up with Megan's hunger for learning. Even at our first lesson, she was able to anticipate what I was going to have her do and did it perfectly.

While it was possible that Megan's gift was only in language, I couldn't help but think that she was more globally gifted. Although her knowledge of English was limited, she used every bit of it to communicate with me. She used gesture, pantomime, and telegraphic speech to get her point across. She was also expert at interpreting what I communicated, whether I used words, gestures, or pantomime.

Just for fun, I gave her some tasks that allowed me to observe how she thought and solved problems. First, I gave her a memory game, the kind where you turn over two cards at a time, looking for the matches. Most first grade children choose cards randomly and deliberate for a long time before they decide which card to turn over. Megan approached the task systematically, working on the top row, left to right, then the next row right to left, and so on. She didn't have a perfect memory for the locations, but her memory was pretty good. I wouldn't want to play against her.

The other thing I did was show her a kids' sudoku puzzle game. There were only four boxes in each row, column, and square, and the game used images instead of numerals. I wasn't able to explain to her that there could only be one of each image in the 2x2 squares, but after she got a couple of answers wrong, she figured out the rule. She was a whiz at Sudoku.

About a week after I read the book *Brown Bear, Brown Bear,*

What do You See? to Megan's class, I carried the book to our lesson. Before our lesson, she looked at the cover and started to recite the book from memory, even though I'd only read it to her class the one time. She read it beautifully when I gave it to her, sounding out the words she didn't know under her breath.

I sat at a lunch table with some of my students while I waited for Megan to finish eating so we could have our lesson. We had been talking about family in class, so it made sense for Naomi to ask if I was a grandmother. When I said no, she asked if I was a mother. Megan spoke up and answered "Yes. Robyn." After our lesson, I checked my planning calendar; it had been three months since the last time I had mentioned my daughter Robyn in class.

That night and over the next few weeks I hit the internet in an attempt to find resources for gifted Chinese students. I finally found a nongovernment organization in Beijing that was working on creating opportunities for gifted students throughout China. However, they didn't offer any programs for students in elementary grades. There was no way I could test Megan for giftedness myself, and, apparently, there was no way to get anyone else to test her. I felt a tremendous sense of responsibility to try to make a difference in Megan's life with whatever time I might have with her. I didn't want her to lose her unique perspective and voice.*

---

* In March, 2023, long after this book was written, but before it was published, I received an email from 16-year-old Megan. She was in high school and was excelling. Her love of English had never faded. She thanked me for the support I had given her. That's why teachers teach.

Chapter 10

Dog Stories

The tiny dog in front of the wall is BJ

WHENEVER THE WATER or pizza delivery guys knocked on my door, Cody barked. He had a deep, fierce-sounding bark. He knew part of his job was to protect our home and the pack, and he took those responsibilities seriously. The men always hid behind my door as I opened it outward, expecting to see a vicious attack dog. Instead, Shadow, the 8-pound frou-frou poodle, would run out to sniff the guy's ankles. The look of bewilderment on their faces was always priceless. I suspected that the pizza place used delivery to my apartment as a kind of hazing or initiation ritual, since I rarely saw the same person twice.

While rearranging my freezer, I picked up a bag of frozen popcorn chicken from the wrong end and one piece dropped to

141

the floor. Shadow got it. I went back into the kitchen, where I was boiling frozen shrimp to make shrimp salad. After I drained it, I found a raw shrimp that had dropped into the burner. I went into the living room and held it out; Cody took it from my hand. I told Shadow, who was too late for the shrimp, "That's okay. You got the chicken, so Cody got the shrimp."

My dogs were spoiled.

One evening, I was sitting on a bench in the courtyard while the dogs were doing doggy stuff when a couple walked up from the street. The woman was obviously intoxicated; the man had his arm around her and was holding onto her arm just to keep her upright. Her head was down, and she clearly had no idea what was happening. I worried that I was seeing the prelude to a drugged sexual assault, but I hoped it was just a man taking his drunken wife/girlfriend home. I thought about intervening, but I couldn't think of any words I could say that would be helpful because I'd have to say them in Chinese. I settled for noting as many details of the two of them as I could, so I could at least be a witness for the woman if anything happened.

Thankfully, the man reappeared soon thereafter, and greeted me with "hello." He was also obviously drunk, but not nearly so impaired as his companion had been. He tried to make conversation with me and didn't stop trying even when I told him repeatedly that I didn't understand. I think he was looking for his car, since he showed me keys and pantomimed driving. He was pacing nervously, talking to me, and edging closer to me with each pace as he spoke.

I did the only thing I could think of to do: I called Cody. Shadow came instead and stared at the man, growling softly. I called Cody again. I think the man realized I had another dog because he moved away from me. Shadow disappeared into the bushes and returned with Cody. The three of us moved to leave. The man, now a safe distance away, called out "Good night." Both dogs turned to watch him.

Instead of running ahead, as he usually did, Cody stayed right beside me until we got to the elevator. I know nothing happened, and maybe I had been perfectly safe the whole time, but I was grateful for having my big, brave dog.

On another occasion, Cody's size almost got him in trouble. An older man was walking his small dog in the courtyard. All the boy dogs flocked to the little girl dog because she was in heat. Shadow was determined to get close to her, as were the other four or five male dogs outside. Cody, by far the biggest dog outside at the time, was interested in playing with all of the dogs, so he was tagging along while the others were trying to mount the little girl.

The man finally recognized that walking a dog in heat where there were other dogs off-leash wasn't a good idea. He scooped up his dog and started to walk toward the far building. All the dogs, including Cody, continued to throng around him as he walked. He tried to nudge them all out of the way, but he was especially concerned about Cody's presence. He seemed afraid Cody would hurt his dog if he tried to mount her, when in truth Cody was trying to play with the other boy dogs. He wasn't even sniffing at the little girl. The man picked up a rock and indicated that he was going to throw it at Cody if Cody made a move toward his dog. I picked up a rock and indicated that I could throw rocks, too.

Meanwhile, two other women and I were following this man, trying to get him to slow down or wait while we picked up our dogs. The man wasn't listening, even though the Chinese women were yelling at him in Mandarin. I was able to explain to the women that Cody wasn't a threat; I used the phrase "he doesn't have" followed by a scissors pantomime, which did the trick. The women laughed and shook their heads. When the man finally stopped moving long enough for us to grab our dogs, one of the women informed the man in Chinese that Cody was neutered and uninterested in his dog. The man dropped his rock and at least had the grace to look embarrassed.

After that event, and now that Shadow was mine, I decided it was time to make an appointment to have him neutered. The vet clinic picked up me and both dogs and transported us to the office; I couldn't take them on the bus, and, given Cody's size, it was unlikely that a taxi would have picked us up. Transportation was apparently an issue lots of their clients faced, so the pickup and drop off service—which included the owner—was not unusual.

I didn't know what the vet's plan was. In America, most vets required the dog to fast for at least a few hours prior to surgery, so they wouldn't vomit while under anesthesia and risk aspirating it. I thought that since our pick-up time was 4:00 p.m., they would examine both dogs, transport me and Cody home, and keep Shadow overnight for surgery the next day. When the doctor took Shadow from me, I asked the interpreter, a vet tech with good English, when I should pick him up, expecting to hear a time the next day. Her response was "30 minutes."

A half hour later, they handed me a groggy Shadow with an incision still oozing blood. The vet showed me how out of it

Shadow was by pulling his tongue out and releasing it like an old-fashioned window shade. He laid Shadow on a desk-height counter where I was sitting.

As Shadow woke up, he started screaming. I'd never heard a dog scream before. I thought he was in pain, but the vet explained in pantomime that Shadow was upset because his body wouldn't respond to his brain's commands, not because of pain from the surgery. I cuddled him like a baby, holding him firmly like he was being swaddled. He still screamed. After about 45 minutes of Shadow's screaming (and my crying), he was able to walk with his leash under him like a sling. Another 15 minutes or so, and he was stable enough for us to leave, though he didn't stop screaming until we were home.

I was pretty sure Shadow would be fine and that I would get over hearing my dog scream—not whimper, not whine—for over an hour. I thought it was barbaric that the dog wasn't sedated while he was coming out of anesthesia, though the vet tech told me that not all dogs reacted the way Shadow had. It was a function of temperament, and Shadow, being the active and bossy little dog he was, would have especially hated feeling helpless. That didn't explain why they didn't sedate him once he started screaming.

The experience was worse for me than it would have been in the States because I wouldn't have seen that whole process; I would have seen Shadow at pick-up time several hours later, if not the next day. For Shadow, I can only assume the process was about the same in either China or America. I have since offered several American vets my appreciation for shielding us pet parents from the suffering of our fur kids.

A small pack of feral dogs frequented my apartment complex courtyard. Whenever we found the pack leader alone, he loved to play Tag with Cody; they would take turns being It. If the other two dogs in the pack were there, though, he would bare his teeth and assume an attack stance. He was obviously protecting his pack, though I couldn't tell if he thought Cody was going to attack them or poach them for a new pack. Since the leader and Cody were buddies, I called the dog Buddy.

I gave the pack food whenever I had leftovers to discard; I had discovered that other residents did the same thing. I wanted to get them a dog house the next time I went to a pet supply store, but I doubted it would be permitted to remain in the courtyard. I toyed with the idea of taking all three of them to the vet for shots, but I didn't know where to find live traps to catch them. I would have loved to have gotten them neutered, but there was no way I could give them the after care they would have needed. I was frustrated at being so unable to help them.

The last time I saw Buddy, he didn't look well. Even though he was alone, he bared his teeth at us. About three days later, Cody and I found Buddy's body under a bush. He had dug a shallow scrape, lay down in it, and died. His front paws were covered with mud from the digging, but the rest of his body was mud-free. Cody sniffed his friend, whined, and looked at me. Cody had seen death before, since he had been in the room when Beowolf had passed away. Shadow sniffed Buddy—who in life wouldn't let the little dog anywhere near him—and bowed to invite him to play. Shadow apparently had no concept of death.

When I got home from work, Buddy was still in the same place. I got my boys and walked to the security guard station. I signaled for one of them to come with me. I couldn't explain what I wanted; all I could do was point to Cody and say "his friend" in Mandarin. The security guard was puzzled, but followed me. The spot that Buddy had chosen not only didn't get foot traffic, but it wasn't visible until you were right there. Poor Buddy didn't get the burial he deserved, but at least the children wouldn't be poking him with sticks.

I was pretty sure Cody and I were the only ones to mourn Buddy. I promised Buddy that I would try to take care of the other two dogs for his sake. I offered a prayer for Buddy, a brown German shepherd mix who took good care of his pack and made at least one friend.

One of Buddy's pack members, an elderly bull mix, went missing after Buddy died. I assumed he had also died, maybe from the same illness Buddy had had. The third member of the pack was still around, though during the winter, his hips and ribs were jutting out. I started feeding him, or rather I started leaving food in one of his hiding places. I assumed he was eating it because his bones stopped showing quite so much. I fed him off and on after that; when I didn't see BJ (Buddy, Jr.) for several days, and I started to see cats in his hiding place, I stopped leaving food. BJ, who looked like a small brown shepherd mix, with black tipping on his fur, black ears and white socks, would reappear a week or so later, and I would resume feeding him. I wanted to catch him and teach him how to be a pet, but he was skittish, even around Cody. There was probably no chance of my catching him without a trap. Every time BJ saw me, he trotted off.

One day I got to observe BJ without his knowing I was there. The dogs and I were just about to go in, so I was half hidden in the doorway. BJ walked over to a new hiding place with a little prance in his gait and his tail wagging. I had only ever seen him fearful before, so it was great to see him looking cheerful and confident. He was so cute!

There was one woman who tried twice to convince me not to leave food out. She knew I wasn't feeding the scraps to my own dogs, but that was about all the communication we could share. Considering the huge feral cat colony we had in residence, I didn't see how anyone could object to my keeping one little dog from starving. I ignored her complaint and continued to care for BJ anyway.

Chapter 11

2014

Cody trying to hide his head under a small table during fireworks

THE SPRING FESTIVAL or lunar New Year is by far the largest and most important holiday of the year in China. It's even bigger than Christmas in the U.S., since Spring Festival is celebrated by everyone, not just those who follow a specific religion. Fireworks stalls popped up all over town in advance of the holiday. The first week after the New Year is another "Golden Week" in China, with almost all businesses closing for the week so that employees are free to visit relatives in other cities. Travel prior to and during that week is chaotic, much like in the U.S. on the Wednesday before Thanksgiving.

The noise of fireworks, usually firecrackers, began in earnest during the last week leading up to the lunar New Year. Strings of little explosions started at 7:00 in the morning and continued throughout the day until about 11:00 at night. As we got closer to New Year's Eve, the familiar sound of *pop! pop! pop!* became more frequent.

The first two years we had lived in China, Cody was a neurotic mess who struggled to deal with the noise of the fireworks. If he was indoors when he heard fireworks, he usually hid in the bathroom; if we were outside, he bolted to the nearest building entrance. By our third Spring Festival, if we were outside and Cody heard explosions, he simply turned around, walked to the door, and waited for me at the elevator. If we were inside, he would calmly walk over to the corner of the room where he could put his head under a little table and hide. Shadow, in contrast, jumped up on the windowsill to see what was happening. Shadow enjoyed watching fireworks, but didn't care about listening to firecrackers; he didn't seem interested in the noise without the light show.

On New Year's Eve, the festivities continued throughout the evening and night. It sounded like being in a war zone, albeit without the risk of injury. The sound of constant fireworks was so loud and so frequent that I couldn't hear the television. I figured *what the heck, if you can't beat 'em, join 'em,* and went downstairs to the courtyard to be part of the festivities. I took Shadow, since he was such a brave little dog, but I left Cody on my bed. I also took two fountain-of-sparks fireworks that I had squirreled away. I lit one firework, but it just burned out, so I went up to a family who were watching and asked them to help me. The four of us, plus the dog in my arms, watched the sparks fly from the second firework. It was pretty, with notes of red, green, and blue flickering among the white sparks. Someone else came out and lit a string of firecrackers. Shadow tried to climb over my shoulder to get away from the noise, so I thought it might be better if we went back in. When I put him down, I discovered that he'd peed down the front of my shirt when the firecrackers went off. Happy New Year!

Red paper in the courtyard, the only casualty of the New Year's fireworks

Around 11:30 that night, I offered to take the dogs outside for a quick walk before bed. Shadow went along happily, but Cody gave me his "are you crazy?" look and hid in the bathroom. The sound finally abated about 5:00 a.m.—or at least that was the last time I was awakened by explosions and whimpers. When we went outside the next morning, the courtyard looked like there had been a battle. I couldn't tell who the opponents had been, but the red paper had clearly lost.

I had become good friends with Molly, one of my former students from the high school, who invited me to share a New Year's lunch with her parents and grandparents. I was convinced that Molly's grandmother made the best dumplings in China. Grandma always made pork and onion dumplings when I was coming, knowing those were my favorite. Aside from having a delicious meal, I always went home with a plastic container filled with homemade dumplings. I deep fried them the next day, the way wontons are fried in American Chinese restaurants, and served them with duck sauce I had brought back from America.

The Lantern Festival was the culminating holiday of the Spring Festival, which began at the new moon with New Year's Day and ended at the full moon, roughly two weeks later. That evening, I again had dinner with Molly, her mother, and her grandparents. Afterwards, we ladies drove to one of the centers of town, leaving Grandpa at home. I had no idea what to expect, and Molly didn't know the right vocabulary to explain it to me.

What I found was essentially a street fair. There were the same games as at any such fair back home: shooting at balloons, tossing bean bags into baskets, and tossing coins at ceramic objects in order to win them. There were the same old food vendors: cotton candy, peanuts, and popcorn. There were some more unusual foods, too, such as sugar-glazed hawthorn apples and "rat-on-a-stick." Just kidding; it was lamb.

Maybe.

There were lighted displays of typical Chinese cultural icons: a bride and groom, the gods from an ancient fable, and various folk tales. The full-sized displays were themselves lanterns, made of colored fabric, presumably silk, and lit from within. There were also sculptures made of lighted ropes or wires. There were several displays of Disney characters dotted here and there, though I doubted they were officially licensed by the Disney Corporation.

I could never get a full explanation of the origin of the Lantern Festival. I thought the holiday itself might have an origin story of its own, independent of the New Year, but all I could learn about the Lantern Festival was that it marked the end of the Spring Festival; maybe that's all the significance the holiday has. To celebrate, people bought inexpensive paper lanterns, shaped rather like hot air balloons, with a small paraffin block suspended on wires at the opening. After the fuel was lit, the balloon filled with hot air and floated away. The people releasing the lanterns made a wish for the coming year while the lanterns, burdened with the wishes, ascended into the heavens.

Molly, her mother, grandmother, and I tried three times to send our lanterns and wishes to heaven. The first lantern was red; we couldn't get the paraffin to light. The second lantern was purple; the burning fuel block fell off and broke into small pieces. The third and last lantern was blue; it took a while, but it finally filled with hot air and lifted off. We watched it drift away, then get caught in a tree, and burst into flames. I hoped our wishes hadn't also crashed and burned.

I had so much fun that night, as if I was a part of China rather than being a visiting foreigner. In the dark, I got fewer stares than usual, even though I didn't see another Western face all evening. It was also nice because Molly's family had apparently adopted me. It was the first time since I had arrived 16 months earlier that I felt like I was home.

School was beginning to feel like home, too. Starting in the second semester, I taught rhythmic movement and folk-dance activities every Thursday. In order to have enough space, my classes met in a large lecture hall/multipurpose room instead of the classrooms. It was a little difficult at first, since the kids weren't used to having as much freedom as being in a large room allowed, but they adapted to the activities and to my expectations. Not only were the lessons a lot of fun, but I was able to see growth in their understanding of both the dances and language from week to week. We worked on a simple circle dance set to an Irish tune which we presented to the second grade on St. Patrick's Day. Paul, the Irish second grade teacher, taught his students a song for the holiday, and they sang it for us.

I also used dance classes to teach the names of body parts and right/left. During R week, I gave the students little plastic rings to place on their right Ring Man finger (R is for right, R is for ring, and R is for Ring Man). I followed up in dance class by having them wear their rings and do the Hokey Pokey, right side only.

A student working on his color words rainbow

R was also for Rainbow, and we had to follow the rainbow to find the leprechaun's pot of gold. I introduced the color green the same week, which was the last color of the rainbow to be introduced. I created a worksheet for the kids that had the rainbow with color words written on each arc. They each got small pieces of colored paper which they used to make a torn paper collage rainbow. The last day of the week, we learned the song "Sing a Rainbow." I loved being able to plan lessons where everything connected to everything else.

During another week, I taught my kids a dance my grandmother had taught me when I was little. I could remember being five or six years old and doing part of the dance with Grandma, while she sat and "helped." She would watch me from her chair and sing with me while I skipped around the room. At five years old, I thought it was cheating for Grandma not to skip with me until the first time I tried to teach it decades later. I started off skipping, but I only got as far as step-hop-step before my heel exploded in intense pain. It wasn't a new injury; I had just aggravated something that had been there for years. I finished the dance by walking and spent the rest of the day limping. I now totally understood why Grandma had sat while I skipped; it was called "getting old."

The foot pain was a reminder of why grey-haired ladies don't skip. Since I was still limping the next morning, I harnessed Cody and took him with me to school. The kids were fascinated by him. Far from being afraid, they all wanted to get close and pet him. When I took Cody for a walk during a break, students came out on all three floors of outside corridors to lean over the balcony and watch. Cody went with me to my two morning classes without any trouble. After I introduced him to the class and let everyone have a chance to pet him, he stayed on a down while I taught the lesson.

Students on balconies watching Cody in the courtyard

The administration was concerned that the students would be frightened of the dog, despite how well the morning had gone. I suspected that the people expressing that concern were more afraid of Cody than the kids were. For the afternoon, he stayed in my boss's office, since all the teachers in my office had class at the same time, and our office would be empty. My afternoon students were extremely disappointed that Cody didn't go to their classes, so we stopped by those classrooms to say goodbye on our way home.

The cutest thing happened while Cody was waiting for me in the office. He was on a down while three guys were in the room talking. When they mentioned my name, Cody picked up his head and whined. Aww! He missed me.

The following summer, Danielle and her partner Nikki asked me to care for Kitty while they traveled to visit Nikki's family in the Philippines. Kitty now had a little sister, Carla, a four-month-old tortoiseshell tabby. Both cats and their parents had stayed at my apartment to take care of the dogs while I had visited America a few weeks earlier, so they all knew each other already. Carla had already shown herself to be a master of being in the most inconvenient place and causing maximum damage with minimum effort, although that might be the definition of "cat."

Carla

It turned out that Kitty was a bit of an a-hole, even by feline standards. After the lights were out at bedtime, Kitty would walk into the bedroom and immediately start growling because the dogs were in there. He didn't understand that if he didn't want to be in a room along with the dogs, he shouldn't walk into a room that already had dogs in it—especially at 5:00 in the morning!

On the other hand, I had to praise Shadow for his restraint. The first night, he didn't handle Kitty's growling well.

First, he barked at the cat, then he jumped off the bed. Jumping off the bed was a no-no because it meant I had to get out of bed to pick him back up. He got one free ride, then spent the rest of the night in his crate if he jumped off again; that was what happened the first night. The next night, Shadow barked a little, but mostly stayed in his spot at the head of the bed. I told him what a good dog he was and offered lots of petting and tummy rubs to compensate for not chasing the cat. He jumped off once, and I reminded him of the rule about spending the night in his crate. He stayed on the bed the rest of the night. He was happy between being told he was a good dog and getting lots of cuddles.

Carla was a much better houseguest than Kitty, except for the part where she crawled on the furniture, knocked my stuff to the floor, and batted it around the room, but what houseguest doesn't do that? She would even sit on the bed with both dogs asleep in their places, as long as they didn't know she was there.

Danielle and Nikki dropped by to visit their cats during a brief pause in their travels. Cody loved both the humans; Danielle was the only other person besides me I had ever seen Cody play with. He played Tug with her, and let her get silly with him, piling toys on his head. Later, he and Carla took their relationship to the next level when they took a nap together on the bed. They were curled up, back-to-back, rather than cuddling, but it was a step in the right direction.

When the following school year started, Megan was no longer my student. However, her teacher and assistant had moved up to the second grade with the class. They already knew me, so I was able to continue working with Megan during lunch. In one of my new first grade classes, I discovered another English prodigy. I was doing a lesson on teddy bears (B is for Bear; B is for Bedtime). My next slide had the caption "Do you have a sleeping friend?" which was totally out of context from what had come before. I heard a little voice read the caption before I could. Needless to say, I found out whose voice it was and talked to the right people to find out how Caleb knew so much English—apparently Caleb's mother spoke to him in English some of the time. It was a tossup whether Caleb's advanced level was due to having had more exposure at an earlier age than his classmates or his being gifted with language; possibly it was both. Regardless of why he was advanced, I decided to include him in the lessons I was doing with Megan. He was a year younger, but more advanced in some ways. A little competition would be good for both of them.

Caleb was excited to have tutoring with me (and Megan). I suspected he would be a lot of fun to work with. When I walked into his classroom the day after inviting him to lessons, he announced, "Today you are beautiful." The kid didn't just know a lot of English; he also knew how to use it.

In October, the teachers and assistants decorated the school for Halloween. We taught our students about Trick-or-Treating, and let them try out the custom at school. The kids enjoyed dressing up and getting candy and treats, even if they didn't have a complete understanding of why they were doing it—though I have to point out that young American students don't know why, either, and no one complains about that.

I choreographed a simple dance to "Monster Mash" for my first graders to present to the other students. Included in the dance were a couple of little hops, which I demonstrated to all five classes as I was teaching the dance. I should have learned from my earlier attempt at skipping that my body was no longer willing to cooperate in such movements, and tried to find a way around hopping; I could have just shifted my weight back and forth to show the move. Unfortunately, I ended up in excruciating pain the next day.

I had had problems on and off with sciatica, which is technically a symptom, not an illness, though I didn't know yet what the underlying cause was. At the same time, I was battling my third cold since the start of the school year. Out of nowhere, I started having nausea and sweats alternating with chills. That was the point at which I told the school I was staying home and asked them to please get me to a doctor.

In contrast to my previous visit to the hospital, this visit was a fuster-cluck. It took place across a Saturday and Sunday. My friend Danielle and a Chinese friend of hers helped me on Saturday, but my boss got called into hospital duty on Sunday to help me. When I say "helped," I mean that they pushed me from place to place on a gurney. Whoever accompanied a patient to a Chinese hospital became the de facto case manager; there were no patient services as we know them in the U.S. There was no one at the hospital whose job was to take a patient from place to place for tests. No one would prepare meals for you in line with your doctor's orders. No one would bathe you or otherwise see to your comfort. Friends and family members had to do all of it. I didn't know what would happen if you went there alone; presumably someone would get around to taking care of you, but I had doubts.

All hospital services had to be paid for in advance by loading money onto the plastic health card; nothing but money was done by computer. We went to one window to put money on my card. Then we were supposed to go to the right specialist for whatever was wrong, but the information desk didn't know where to send me. I obviously had a cold, but that wasn't the problem. I appreciated that in the U.S. we first saw a generalist who could order a broad range of tests to try to figure out where the problem was before trying to consult a specialist. Of course, it also helped that U.S. doctors spoke English.

Doctors' notes were handwritten into little books that the patient had to buy. The book resembled the blue book exam booklets I had had to buy as an undergrad. If the patient forgot to carry their book with them from home, they had to buy a new one, which meant that the doctors had no history or way to find out what had gone before. I ended up in the gastrointestinal clinic. The doctor wrote his observations and any tests he recommended in my little paper book. Then we had to wander hither and yon paying for those tests on my hospital card and then getting them done. When the tests were finished, we picked up the results; the patient owned the actual test results, whether they were lab reports or films. Once we had all the papers, we returned to the doctor, who examined the information and theoretically should have pronounced a diagnosis.

That didn't happen; instead, the doctor referred me to another clinic within the hospital.

One huge difference between American and modern Chinese medicine was that in China they didn't treat the symptoms, only the underlying illness. If treating the illness also happened to alleviate the symptoms, well then, weren't you lucky! Pain was a symptom. So was nausea. Finally, one doctor recognized that I needed something for pain, even without knowing its cause. We went to the pharmacy to get the medication he prescribed, and then we went to the Injections Office to get the medication injected. I had to think that it would have been more efficient, and less jarring, to leave me, as a patient, in one place and let people come to me. Maybe not more efficient, but more humane.

I spent parts of two days at the hospital, searching for a diagnosis, but I never did get one. The list of all the parts that had been ultra-sounded, scanned, prodded, poked, and beaten on and that were not causing the problem included my appendix, ovaries, kidneys, and lumbar disks. The best guess was that this was a major sciatic attack caused by bone spurs on the vertebrae; the other symptoms were most likely an unrelated viral infection. I went home not knowing anything more than I had before the fuster-cluck had started.

I took the two bags of scans and doctors' notes that I had accumulated to my acupuncturist, so he had all the latest information. He was able to alleviate the pain within a few sessions, though the treatment continued for several weeks. I also bought a heating pad, or rather an electric hot water bottle, which I alternated with a bag of frozen veggies. Cody and Shadow camped out on the sofa with me for the next few days, binge-watching Star Trek: The Next Generation.

When I returned to school, my boss wanted me to rehearse and maybe re-choreograph the Monster Mash dance my students were doing for our Halloween celebration. He didn't seem to understand why I had been absent for a week. I decided that at the end of the school year, it would be time for me to leave China and get back to American health care.

Before I returned to school, but after I was able to walk comfortably again, I put my boys in the elevator to go outside. Cody was off-leash, as usual for daytime walks in the courtyard. Shadow and I had gotten off the elevator and walked to the door when I realized that Cody wasn't with us; he must have stayed on the elevator, and the doors closed him in. Shadow and I rang for the elevator; when it opened, there was no Cody. We got back into the elevator and stopped at every floor to call Cody's name and listen for a response. We got off when I thought I heard Cody answer me. I didn't see him, so I pushed the button for the elevator again. When it opened, Cody was in there—alone. I have no idea what happened or how he had gotten back on the elevator. Could he have pushed the button? I knew that everyone at the complex knew him; many people greeted him by name when we went outside. Maybe someone had put him in, assuming I'd find him. Either way, Cody looked as relieved to see me as I was to see him.

As I started planning my slide shows for November, I learned that it was almost impossible to find a good graphic for a November calendar if the country you were in didn't celebrate Thanksgiving. I wanted to teach about the holiday, but I wasn't sure I would be allowed to; it was part of our contracts that we wouldn't talk about religion or politics with our students, that we would respect China's religious beliefs (officially atheism), and that we would refrain from engaging in religious or political activity. In some ways, Thanksgiving was more religious than Christmas, Easter, or Passover; after all, to whom were those thanks being offered?

The activities I did combined what any PreK/K class would do in the States with lessons specifically for cultural awareness. For example, I told my students that Americans do three things on Thanksgiving: say "thank you" for everything they have—since a lesson on counting blessings would be awkward in an atheistic country—eat special foods—without getting into questions about gluttony—and visit family.

I had the students draw pictures of what they were thankful for and trace/write the sentence "I am thankful for ..." under the picture. What struck me was that their pictures were of the same things that American students at that age would draw: parents, siblings, teachers, pets, and best friends. That told me that they understood what the "thank yous" were about.

For the day of the actual holiday, I baked some cornbread and made applesauce, enough for each of my students to have about a cubic inch of bread and a tablespoon of applesauce. We graphed their reaction to the new foods with smiley faces and frowny faces and counted how many liked or disliked each of the foods.

Once Thanksgiving had passed, I started adding bits of Christmas lore into my lessons. In China, Christmas was observed solely as a secular holiday. I used my lesson time on three successive Fridays in December to show a video of *The Nutcracker Ballet* in its entirety. I wasn't sure the kids would understand or appreciate the art form, but on the subsequent Thursdays, when I said I'd see them tomorrow, they would ask about the ballet and cheer when I said yes, we'd watch it. One of the classroom assistants told me that ballet was rare in China. I thought that was a shame since ballet and traditional Chinese dance share some characteristics; both are graceful dance forms with rigid and stylized movements in unique combinations.

Shoes on Christmas morning, 2014

I had returned to Maryland to celebrate with my family the Christmas before, so getting to teach my students the joy of Santa was my consolation prize for not being able to go home this year. The best part of believing in Santa Claus is being a co-conspirator in bringing the magic of Santa to someone else. I explained to my children that in some countries, children put their shoes out for Santa. We wrote letters to Santa in class. The assistants who supervised the children in the dorms helped them put their shoes in the hall on Christmas Eve, with their letters inside.

On Christmas morning, the kids woke up to find gift-wrapped pieces of candy in their shoes. (Guess who?) Merry Christmas!

Chapter 12

2015

Cody's girlfriend Remi

BOTH SCHOOLS I taught at in China celebrated the solar New Year, January 1, with talent shows featuring students and staff. I participated in the talent show at the high school, singing a lullaby I had written for Robyn when she was three years old. At the boarding school, I was part of the audience when the students presented a celebration of the arts in honor of the New Year. Most of the performances were only a minute long, though some lasted up to five minutes. The acts included singers, instrumentalists, and dancers, either solo or in combinations up to a whole class.

Many of the students showed impressive talent, especially those who played musical instruments like drums, piano, or traditional Chinese instruments. There were some beautiful dance pieces, including a traditional Chinese dance with fans presented by the teaching assistants. Martha, one of my students, danced a highly stylized traditional Chinese dance while another student sang. I could imagine Martha becoming a professional dancer; her grace and interpretation of dance gave her performance an almost ethereal quality, even at the age of seven.

This talent show included one of the most unique performance pieces I had ever seen. One of the instrumentalists played traditional Chinese music as background to a visual artist who created sand drawings, projected onto a screen so the audience could see her work. I couldn't begin to describe how incredibly gifted the young artist was or how well her images blended with the music. She created image after image with such subtlety and economy of movement that I found myself waiting with bated breath for the next picture.

I was frustrated by having to leave this job at the end of the semester. Everyone that I came in contact with in my daily activities—teachers, assistants, and students—had nothing but praise for my work. My students were making good progress. The Chinese ESL teachers and I had started some tentative collaboration. The elementary school principal, who had observed my classes on occasion but couldn't speak English, had posted a video of my lessons on the school website. There was only one person who wasn't happy with me: my immediate supervisor. Given Chinese attitudes toward hierarchies—i.e. the higher-ranking person is always right—there was no way for me to remain there. Instead, I took a temporary position in a private language school to finish out the school year and my time in China.

A new couple moved into the apartment complex. The most notable thing about them was that they had three dogs: two big golden retrievers and a Pomeranian/corgi mix. We usually walked our dogs around the same time, and the dogs seemed to get along well.

Mei Ling and me

Mei Ling, the female half of the couple, spoke English as well as I spoke Chinese—or as badly. She and Liu Jie, her partner, understood more English than I understood of Chinese, though. We started off communicating about the dogs, using gestures and single words, but soon we were able to progress beyond that. I liked their friendliness, especially hers, so I experimented with different ways to communicate. One of the most effective was using texting and translating apps on our phones while we sat outside and watched our dogs play. Of course, the best teacher for any foreign language is the need to communicate, so Mei Ling was teaching me Chinese, while I was teaching her English, and we both shared lots of laughter along the way.

Shortly after we met, Mei Ling added another dog to her pack—Remi, an Old English sheepdog. Cody loved to play with all of Mei Ling's dogs, but Remi was his favorite. Shadow liked the little pom/corgi, but he wasn't crazy about the two goldens or Remi.

Soon after being adopted, Remi went into heat. Remi liked Cody, not caring that he had been neutered many years ago. Cody had to fight off one of the goldens in order to earn the right to, um, 'play' with Remi. Unfortunately, while neutering didn't prevent his starting the process, it did keep him from being able to finish. Evidently, he thought he could just give up and walk away, and was surprised to find that there was a part of him still attached.

Mei Ling and I made ourselves comfortable on a bench to

wait for nature to deflate the problem. The young golden, Doh-Gee, kept trying to make it a threesome, even jumping over the two dogs where they were joined. Cody had to fight him off again, something that seemed especially difficult when he and Remi were still attached. Shadow kept trying to mount Remi's legs, since that was all he could reach. Eventually, everything returned to normal, such as it was.

My friendship with Mei Ling was slow to develop. We were like two moms of toddlers, meeting now and then at the park, with the complication of a language barrier. Our conversations were always a mixture of English and Chinese. As my Chinese improved, as the weather warmed, and as my free time increased, we became friends. When Cody was injured by jumping off the bed and landing wrong, Mei Ling and Liu Jie came to our apartment to visit him, bringing gifts and Remi with them.

One evening, Mei Ling and Liu Jie invited us to walk to the park with them. It was not a dog park, per se, but after dark, no one else was there. We had six dogs, including my two. Other people came by, so that we usually had seven dogs playing at any one time. One of the other dog owners was Dr. Liu, a medical doctor. His spoken English was limited, though his understanding seemed pretty good. I enjoyed meeting him, though Cody and two of Mei Ling's dogs ganged up on his golden retriever.

A few nights later, I sent Mei Ling a message that we were in the courtyard. Instead of joining us downstairs, she texted back an invitation for us to go up to her place. I was surprised to learn that Mei Ling and Liu Jie actually had ten dogs, though most of them were small dogs who were crated while we were there. Dr. Liu was there with his golden retriever, so with my dogs there were thirteen dogs in the apartment. Fortunately, they had the top floor apartment, which meant they had a second floor with a large rooftop area.

It was a lot of fun to converse in two languages at once, at least with people who wanted to learn and communicate, and weren't worried about grammar. There was a lot of shared laughter, which made it feel pretty risk-free to make mistakes.

Dr. Liu and I were invited back for Chinese BBQ the following night. The human guests included a friend of Liu Jie's and his girlfriend, Mei Ling's younger brother, as well as Dr. Liu and me. We also had six dogs for company: my two and Mei Ling's four personal pets. I gathered that her other six were fosters. Liu Jie was studying to be a vet. Their dream was to open a clinic and shelter for dogs, though it seemed to me that they already had the shelter part going on in their living room.

The evening was filled with good food and even better company; everyone was stuffed. It was the sort of meal where you ate for a while, talked, started eating again, and suddenly it was 11:00. No one spoke good English (well, except me), but everyone spoke a little. Among them, they were mostly able to communicate with me. When all else failed, we could text each other and use the built-in translators.

Dr. Liu was either a neurosurgeon or a professor of neuro-surgery; maybe he was both. He was also funny when he got drunk. He started expounding on ancient Chinese poetry and how it could be interpreted in so many ways. He first translated the poem he was talking about into English and recited it to me, before launching into a lengthy discourse in Chinese. The poem was interesting. As best I could remember, it said:

> *You say you love the rain,*
> *But you open your umbrella*
> *When it rains.*
> *You say you love the sun,*

Cody

But you stand in the shadow
When the sun shines.
You say you love the wind,
But you close your window
When the wind blows.
This is why I am afraid
When you say you love me.

I wished I could understand what Dr. Liu had to say about it, though I suspected drunken discourse sounded the same no matter what language it was in.

Cody kept complaining because Remi was more interested in food than in him. Shadow was social, and not just because he was trying to get food. He let people hold him and pet him. That evening, he definitely preferred women to men, but I noticed that the women held him like a baby, up to their shoulders, while the men just set him on their laps. He growled only one time, when I had just taken a bone from him, and a man tried to pick him up at almost the same moment. That was quite an improvement for him. I was hopeful that maybe someday soon I could stop telling people he was a naughty dog.

Remi's puppies

A few days later, I learned that Remi, Cody's girlfriend, was pregnant. Of course, Cody was neutered and couldn't be the father, but I wasn't sure how to break the news to him. When it was time, Remi had twelve babies, but two died at or before birth, leaving her with 10 healthy pups. All of them were black, with some small markings in white. I took Cody over to visit mother and babies. Dr. Liu's golden was the putative father, but since he was young and irresponsible,

169

we told Cody—a more mature and stable dog—that they were his puppies. He had always loved baby critters, so he was probably happy to be their dad. Sadly, Cody only enjoyed a few weeks of fatherhood before we had to leave China.

The big day for fireworks in China was the eve of the lunar New Year. Stalls went up all over town with a wide variety of fireworks for sale. I finally planned ahead and bought two big boxes of fireworks during the Spring Festival to save for the 4th of July, 2015.

When the holiday rolled around, I let my neighbors know that I would be setting off fireworks at about 9:00 p.m. When the time came, there was a crowd of people in the courtyard. While one friend was setting up the two boxes, I passed out sparklers to the kids. We all stood back to watch the first box. Inside the box were about 20 tubes, each one with a different kind of firework. They fired in sequence once the fuse was lit, building from a fountain of sparks to things that shot into the air. The finale was a sky full of wonderful, sparkling stars.

We lit the second box and watched it happen all over again.

After all my fireworks were used up, people started retrieving their secret stashes of fireworks, including some that were unusually pretty. Some, of course, were just loud. My bilingual friends made sure that everyone knew why we were setting off fireworks. By now, I had celebrated Independence Day in France, Italy, and China, as well as the U.S.

My last Fourth of July in China was one of the all-time best. We would soon be heading back to the U.S. for a new adventure.

Chapter 13

Mostly About Shadow

Shadow as an older dog

WHEN SHADOW HAD FIRST COME to live with me in August, 2013, he had had no manners. He was excitable, snappy, and not house trained. Within three weeks of his arrival, my neighbors were already commenting that he was a mean little dog. While he was adorable, he could be irritable and was likely to nip at fingers when he was annoyed. The groomers told me he had tried to bite them, though luckily they were willing to continue grooming him. When I did something Shadow didn't like, he would retaliate by pooping in the apartment. I called him a "spite pooper." There were a couple of months when I thought he'd be going back to join his "dad" in Boston, until it turned out to be too expensive to ship him. Once Shadow became mine, I started training him in earnest. For a long time, I had to warn my neighbors that he wasn't a "good dog." They wanted to approach him because he was so little and cute, while sweet, gentle Cody scared them because he was so big.

Cody's hoard of 5 toys

However, one of the nicest things about having Shadow in the house was that he taught Cody how to play with toys. Cody's early life and trauma apparently hadn't exposed him to much play; even though he had had access to toys since coming to live with me, he had never shown any interest in toys beyond destroying them. Interactive play seemed beyond him. Once the toys became valuable to Shadow, though, Cody started to be interested in them, although mostly to hoard them and keep them away from Shadow. Cody usually took toys to the sofa to chew on them gently and make them squeak, whereas Shadow took his toys to a rug beside my desk, where he gave them death shakes.

One evening, Cody took a toy from Shadow's stash in my office to his spot on the sofa. A few minutes later, Shadow came running into my office with the same toy in his mouth; Cody was right behind him. When Shadow dropped the toy on the rug, Cody picked it up and started squeaking it. Shadow stood behind him, jumping at his back legs. Cody eventually settled on the rug to chew on the toy, with Shadow climbing all over him.

Many of my neighbors were afraid of my dogs. Some refused to get into the elevator when we were in there; some even got out of the elevator when we got in. I couldn't explain to them that big, scary Cody was more frightened than they were, and even feisty Shadow didn't bite, though I wasn't sure the groomer would have agreed. I watched these people take ridiculous measures (and lots of stairs) to avoid my perfectly safe dogs.

One morning, we passed a father and 10-year-old daughter on our walk. The father was fine with the dogs, but the girl became flustered and moved to the far side of the walkway. As she passed, she made a "shoo" noise and gesture directed toward Shadow. Shadow, always up for a game, barked back at her with one loud poodle-bark that scared the crap out of her. She shrieked and scurried back behind her father. I scolded him, even though I thought it was a well-deserved bark.

I took the boys out for their afternoon walk, with Shadow on-leash and Cody off. Shadow and I walked over to the trash cans so I could throw a bag away. When we started to walk back to the play area, we saw Cody, surrounded by little girls who were petting him. I was surprised both that Chinese children were interacting with my big dog—considering how much their parents seemed to fear him—and even more surprised that Cody was allowing it.

The oldest of the girls walked over to Shadow and me. She sat on a bench and started petting Shadow, who started wriggling in delight. She carefully picked him up and set him on her lap to pet him. One or two of the other girls petted him, too, but they were afraid of getting licked. Shadow succeeded in licking the nose of the girl who was holding him, which made her giggle. Just before we went in, the girls tried to pet Cody again, but this time he was too fast for them and ran away. I think the girls and the various parents and grandparents were surprised to realize that Cody was avoiding them.

I bought a stepladder to let Shadow control when he got on and off the bed. First, I had to teach him to climb it. He was food motivated, so I started with little bits of pepperoni. I placed one at the front edge of the bottom step. I had to wave the piece under his nose and let him see where I put it, coax him in my sweetest voice, and threaten to let Cody have the treat before Shadow finally took it. After that, he progressed quickly. I stopped the training session when he was standing with both front paws on the step and eating a treat from the back of the step. I could safely leave treats on the stepladder for Shadow because Cody would never eat Shadow's treat. It wasn't a question of canine ethics; I knew Cody would avoid that big, scary, strange, new, red stepladder for several weeks or months, no matter how many treats I put on it.

When I took the dogs out for a bedtime walk, Shadow suddenly froze and growled softly, his attention on something inside one of the apartment building entrances. The thing that had his attention stepped outside; it was a man. Shadow started barking and growling much more loudly. The man was startled, especially when Cody, who was not on a leash, came running over and added his bark. I called Cody back, but I didn't scold Shadow. He almost never barked at people, only dogs. The man walked away, poking his head into each entrance of the building. The dogs and I followed him, with Shadow offering canine commentary. The man ended up standing and watching the usual crowd playing chess inside the front lobby. I wondered if he had been plotting something when our presence thwarted him. I wanted to ask the men playing and watching if they knew the man Shadow was barking at, but they seemed intent on the game. If my dogs felt suspicious of someone, so did I. Safely back in my apartment, I double-locked my door and removed my spare key from its hiding place, just in case.

Shadow (r) and friend

Shadow did not work or play well with others, humans or dogs. Although he was interested in other dogs, he usually just barked at them. The few times I had let him off his leash to play with another dog, he had quickly lost interest in playing and instead explored the freedom he had suddenly gained. Therefore, it was quite exciting when he saw another toy poodle outside and wanted to play; I let him off his leash to see what would happen. The two poodles seemed to recognize each other as brothers. The other dog was slightly larger and more beige than white, but they resembled each other enough that all the kids and grandparents on the playground stopped to watch the two little dogs frolicking.

One day Ruby, a neighbor from the building across the courtyard, was outside with her young son and a box containing a baby chick and a duckling. It took a little while for the dogs to notice the babies, so Ruby and I talked as we watched the birds wander around the yard, sticking together like they were twins. When Cody saw the baby birds, he got excited. Given that Cody was the dog that had helped rescue a litter of baby bunnies when he'd lived with me only a couple of months, I wasn't worried that he'd hurt them. However, I decided to be extra cautious. I picked up the chick and let him sniff it. Cody was very respectful. After he got one sniff, he tried to get more, but I didn't want to scare the birds. Then Shadow saw them. He was pretty restrained, for Shadow. He got close enough to smell them without getting close enough to touch them. Good boy!

Then he peed on the grass they were hiding in. Typical Shadow move.

Two girls walking Shadow

By the time we were ready to leave China, I could say that Shadow was a good dog. He wasn't 100% of the way to where I wanted him to be, but he was at least 70% of the way there, and maybe more. He allowed people to pet him. He allowed people he knew to pick him up, though he might still wiggle to get down. He understood English, but he would still respond to Chinese when he heard it. Shortly before our departure date, two girls asked if they could walk Shadow around the courtyard. I gave them his leash; he was an angel.

I could have found Shadow a home in China; Mei Ling would have adopted him, if nothing else. However, I couldn't imagine leaving Shadow behind. I worked with a pet relocation service in Beijing to transport all of us, plus our luggage, from Zibo to Beijing. They arranged for all the travel documents the dogs would need to enter the U.S., as well as for shipping Shadow as unaccompanied cargo. Cody, of course, would travel as my service dog. Ultimately, the entire cost of getting both dogs back to the U.S. was $4,000.

The relocation agency sent a car and driver to Zibo to transport us to Beijing. Shadow stayed at the veterinarian's office, while Cody and I went to a hotel. We all met at the vet's office the next morning to begin the health certificate process. I asked the vet tech if Shadow had bitten anyone yet, but he had apparently learned to inhibit that behavior; I was relieved. They did tell me that he was "active." Shadow was amazingly smart for a toy poodle, but he was as wiggly as any small dog.

Meanwhile, I could see how different Cody was. He hadn't left Zibo since our arrival nearly three years earlier. I didn't have him in his harness because I didn't need his help in the hotel or at the vet, but to forestall questions, I had him in his training vest. When we got to wherever we were going, he automatically put himself on a "down," without my saying anything. He was much more agreeable to being petted by strangers, especially women; he sometimes even let men pet him. As we walked, he responded to my directions. One of his weak areas was staying on a down when I moved away from him, but after a couple of meals in the hotel restaurant where I visited the buffet, he didn't feel the need to check on me unless I was out of sight.

I taught Cody how to walk through a revolving door; I got the impression that he actually liked the challenge of having to time his movements. Training him to ride in elevators had been a real issue before we moved to China, but he'd been riding in them at least three times a day for 33 months. When the elevator at the hotel opened, Cody hesitated until I said "elevator," then he walked right in. The hotel had floor-to-ceiling mirrors in some spots, and Cody kept stopping to look at his reflection. I couldn't tell if he thought it was another dog or if he recognized himself.

Our trip home went well. Cody wasn't exactly calm during

the flight from Beijing to Detroit, but he behaved well. In fact, most of the flight crew, including the pilot, made friends with Cody, and made a point to say goodbye to him after we landed. He actually seemed to like the flight from Detroit to Baltimore, and made new friends there. Shadow flew alone the next day, but he arrived safe and sound and was happy to see me. The dogs were happy to see each other again, which was heart-warming to watch.

Monkey wearing an outfit I brought her from China. She later gleefully destroyed it.

We all stayed with Robyn and Michael, Robyn's new husband, for the first week. Monkey and Cody obviously recognized each other. They picked up right where they had left off three years earlier, with Monkey enthusiastically humping Cody's head. However, there were some frictions among the four critters in the house (three dogs and a cat), leading someone to express their displeasure scatalogically. Fortunately, my parents invited me and Shadow to stay with them, while Cody remained with Robyn.

It was amusing to watch my parents with Shadow. My dad had always liked both dogs and cats; he and my biological mother had had both during their brief marriage. Mom, who was technically my stepmother, was totally a cat person. While we were staying at their home, though, they both treated Shadow like their baby. Shadow was already a fat little poodle, but they were giving him so many treats that I worried I might not be able to fit him under the plane seat when we flew out.

During the three and a half weeks that we were traveling

between jobs and homes, I spent hours catching up on health-care for all of us, visiting the doctor, dentist, and vet. I was based in Maryland, but also made time to visit my mother in North Carolina. I emptied my storage unit into one that was bigger and cheaper, taking out those things I wanted to ship ahead. There was a lot to accomplish in a short period of time.

Chapter 14

Alaska: The Last Frontier

An aerial view of Atka (photographer unknown)

ONCE I KNEW I needed to return to the U.S. in order to have access to American healthcare, I had started searching for a new job. I didn't want to return to teaching in normal mainstream America as I still didn't know why I had never been successful in past positions. Until I could figure that out, I was afraid to teach in a public school again. I looked for jobs that were somewhat different from what I had always done. The only public school teaching positions I applied to were in the Alaskan Bush—in Alaska, "bush" refers to any area that can't be accessed by the state road system. In June, 2015, I signed a contract to teach at a school that was essentially a two-room school house; I would be the only teacher for the secondary students while another teacher would work with the elementary students.

My new school was in the Aleutians, that chain of islands that juts out from the southwest corner of Alaska and points toward Asia. I would be located on Atka, the next to the last inhabited Aleutian island. We were so far west that we were actually in a different time zone from the rest of Alaska. In order to get there, I would first fly to Anchorage, where the school district office was located. That would give me a chance to meet the administrative people I would be answering to. I would also have a chance to buy groceries and supplies to ship to the school, since the only store on the island was more like a large convenience store than a supermarket. Then, I would take a three-hour flight on a 36-passenger plane to Dutch Harbor/Unalaska, where I could purchase perishables. Finally, the next day, I would board a 10-person plane for the 1.5-hour flight.

As it turned out, the last plane could carry up to 10 passengers, but only if they had reservations; the flight crew only installed as many seats as they needed for the trip. Our last flight had four rows of two seats, and every seat was filled. Shadow's carrier didn't fit under the seat, so he was where my feet should have been, while I sat sideways. Poor Cody had to lie in the aisle. I had to give Cody two pills to calm him down, even though the prescription said just one-half of a pill. Fortunately, the other passengers kept reaching out to pet and comfort him. Luckily, the flight only took an hour and a half, and we arrived with no problems.

The plane landed in what looked like a parking lot, especially because there were more than a dozen people and vehicles waiting there. The kids were interested in the dogs, and I let one of them hold Cody's leash. After a few squabbles over whose turn it was to walk the dog, Cody dug his feet in, lay down, and refused to walk for any of them. Poor Cody! He'd had a rough day.

Jay, the school district's maintenance man, took me for a tour of the village in the car that the school district had just purchased. The buildings were as run down and shabby looking as any beach town, though the salt air and winds were responsible for that. However, things seemed to be in good repair, for all that the exteriors looked questionable.

The District provided me with a three-bedroom house to rent, but it couldn't have existed as a house in the lower 48 because none of the bedrooms had closets. One room had an open unit of white wire shelving, but a different room had the "master bedroom" furniture. I figured I'd see how much furniture-shifting I could do on my own over the weekend, though I was sure I could always get Jay to help if I had to.

Buddy, Jay's dog and Kartuufilax/Scamp's father

Most of the 60-70 permanent residents lived in what was essentially a single cul-de-sac. A handful of residents, mostly elders, lived in the 'old' village, which also housed many of the community's older buildings. Dogs mostly stayed in the village; Jay's dog, Buddy, ran free, but was usually within sight or sound of Jay. There weren't any strays, nor was there any veterinary care. Troublesome dogs or dogs that were suffering were all dealt with the same way—a bullet to the head. Cody and Shadow had both lived on the streets as strays, so I knew they were capable of running free safely, but they hadn't done it while also having a loving home. One of the things I had to do was train them to be island dogs.

For the first day or two, I walked both dogs on leashes; I figured first they needed to learn where home was. Once they seemed to know that, I started letting Cody off the leash, staying outside where he could see me. His rule, just as it had been in China, was that he had to respond when I called him. He learned that he just needed to show me where he was. Usually, I would call Cody's name, and he would lift his head up from behind a dune and look at me. I would say "thank you," and he would go back to whatever he was doing. He went farther and farther at each walk. Finally, he was gone long enough that I went back home without waiting for him.

There were three doors between the outside and the living area of my house. The first door opened into what functioned as an airlock, shielding the rest of the house from cold, wind, and rain. The second door opened into a mud room, with shelving for winter wraps and a big chest freezer. The third door opened into the living room/kitchen. When I went into the house and left Cody outside, I left the airlock door open so Cody could at least get in out of the weather. In theory, he would bark to alert me to his presence, but he apparently didn't get the memo on that part. Instead, he would enter the airlock space, and wait quietly for me to open the door. Or he would leave because I didn't open the door right away. I usually heard him enter, but not always. We kept working on that system until we got it right. "Getting it right" meant hanging a string of bells from a door-knob and teaching Cody to ring for me to let him in.

A waterfall on Atka

The weather was usually rainy in the morning, overcast by midday, and raining again overnight, though I was lucky to arrive on the first of a string of clear, sunny days. The beauty of the island was not overstated by the people who had recruited me. There were snow-capped mountains (in August!), black sand beaches, tundra grasses, and even a few waterfalls. I learned that most of the electricity on the island was generated by the running water. There were few trees anywhere on the island. I couldn't wait to get out and explore.

When the next morning dawned bright and sunny, I took Shadow for a walk to the beach. Cody was busy doing whatever dogs do, but he joined us later. I found a place to sit and just enjoyed the sights and sounds of the beach. Right below my perch was one of the mountain springs, making its way to the ocean. It formed a stream, with little rapids as it flowed over the rocks, and created a large pool which was filled with lots of fish. I didn't see them well enough to describe them, let alone identify them, though they kept breaching the surface of the water. I thought I saw two of them playing the fish equivalent of Tag. Past the pool, the stream had split to form an oxbow. After that, it ran straight to the ocean. What with the stream, the ocean, the birds, and the fish, there was plenty to amuse me for an hour or so. It was wonderful just to watch and be.

There were no animals on the island that posed a danger to humans: no bears or wolves, though there were foxes. Since most of the dogs were Cody's size, the foxes on the island were not a danger to them. If Cody had had to, he could have taken a fox in a fight. Shadow, the little frou-frou poodle? Not so much. Most dogs only faced one danger: humans on ATVs. Fortunately, ATVs made a lot of noise, and most dogs were smart enough to get out of the way.

This bald eagle let me get as close as 10 feet to get this picture.

Then there were the birds, mostly bald eagles and ravens. I had people tell me that eagles didn't eat dogs, they only wanted fish. Then the next person would announce that I needed to keep an eye on Shadow lest an eagle carry him off. I couldn't figure out whom to listen to, and finally decided to follow the advice of the one guy who seemed to know what he was talking about. He said that as long as the salmon were running, the eagles wouldn't be interested in a dog. However, if the eagles started to go hungry, I would need to hold onto Shadow.

Shadow wasn't happy about being left behind when Cody

would take off for parts unknown. I knew that I had a responsibility to keep him safe, but he was also a dog; I had some responsibility to let him act like one. I started letting Shadow off the leash, but following where he went so that he was never far from me. It turned out that he didn't want to go far off anyway; the world is big and scary when you're little. Shadow would start to follow Cody, but turn back toward me when Cody got too far away from home. Shadow also seemed to understand that he was outside for potty purposes; he came in as soon as he was done, and he didn't try to come in before he was finished. Both boys were well on their way to living the doggy dream. They had as much freedom as they wanted, plus meals, soft beds, and all the tummy rubs they could handle.

Sonja, my teaching partner, was a slender, red-headed vegan from Reno. She finally arrived on Thursday, a week after I did. She had been stranded in Dutch Harbor since the previous Sunday, since the airline had canceled the flight on three consecutive days. Immediately upon her arrival, we had a conference call with all the other employees of the school district: the superintendent, the teachers at our sister school in Adak, and the business manager at the office in Anchorage. Among other things, we were told that according to state law, all students in Kindergarten and 7th grade had to have TB tests.

On Friday, I drove Sonja around for a tour of the village. Our destination was the clinic, to introduce ourselves to the community health nurse there and arrange for the TB tests. I found visiting the clinic to be an interesting experience and quite an education in rural health care. The nurse worked under the direction of a doctor who was not in residence. She took histories and performed routine exams and tests. She sent all the gathered information to the supervising physician, who gave orders for treatment, including prescriptions. The consultations took place via phone, fax, or online. Medications were available for acute illnesses, but no prescription medications were available for chronic conditions. All the medications were under lock and key, dispensed by a machine.

The community health nurse told us she could only offer care for wellness and chronic conditions to Alaskan Natives and Native Americans. The nurse was quick to assure us that we would be cared for in the event of an acute illness or an accident, but that we had to go elsewhere to find a primary care provider. I couldn't even get a TB test without paying the full, uninsured rate for it, though having just come from China and being new to the school system, I probably should have had one.

Sonja and I both planned to stay for multiple years, unless we found that there was something we couldn't tolerate. The weather in the winter could have been a deal-breaker, but neither of us would know until we went through it once. However, we were both over 50. Sonja was in better health than I was overall, but at our age, things were starting to wear out. It bothered me to think that being a resident of the island, as well as a member of the community, didn't entitle me to use the only health care facility on the island. We wouldn't learn until the following April that the community health nurse had been mistaken; the local clinic's funding included a mandate to serve all residents on the island, regardless of ethnicity. Fortunately, the issue never came up.

My class had eight students in grades 5-12, while Sonja's had six students in grades K-2. I was usually most comfortable with the younger students. Sonja, on the other hand, had never worked in an early childhood classroom; most of her experience had been with secondary students. Each of us was working outside our comfort zone. We talked about trading jobs, but we both had reasons for wanting to do the exact job we were doing. Since we each had expertise the other lacked, though, we found built-in mentors in each other.

Sonja and I both came from a special education background. We were politically liberal and shared an irreverent sense of humor. We were each single moms with beloved daughters. We were also both animal lovers with lots of room for pets in our homes and hearts. We would remain friends long after our time together as colleagues ended.

We decided that Sonja would teach P.E. to all the students, while I would teach them fine arts—music, drama, and visual art. Neither of us taught our subjects in the way the kids expected. I taught Art, for example, with a heavy dose of Art History mixed in; Sonja's P.E. classes included yoga, meditation, and martial arts.

Sam

Sam was Sonja's dog. I thought he looked like a hound except for his color. He was an active dog, so he and Shadow got along pretty well. He was also a bigger dog, so he and Cody got along, too. To be honest, Sam got along with everyone; the first day that Sonja adopted an orange kitten, the cat leaped around playing with Sam's tail while Sam just grinned.

I occasionally saw Sam staring from the window of Sonja's house at some of the kids as they passed by on their way to school. He wasn't barking, just watching the kids. If my door was open, Sam would walk into my house to visit my dogs. He was also willing to take care of any stray dog cookies I might have had lying around; I taught him to catch them midair as I tossed them. Sometimes my dogs went to Sam's house and asked Sonja if Sam could come out to play. Between Sam and Buddy, Cody and Shadow had friends to play with.

I loved watching Cody head off to explore the tundra with his tail out and his nose up. The difference in his demeanor from when we lived in Baltimore to living on the island was striking; it was even more striking when I compared Cody with "the quivering mass of dog flesh" that I had first met nine years earlier. Time and patience, plus consistent and persistent training, had created an environment in which Cody

Cody among the tundra grasses

had flourished. He had learned not only to trust me, but also to trust himself. He had learned when to be cautious and when to ignore his fears. He had learned to choose what he wanted to do and how, while still remaining a loyal and protective member of a pack. Living on an isolated, remote, and safe island, Cody's happiness and independence became complete.

Our school district used a standards-based curriculum. Students progressed through the grades by demonstrating mastery of the standards. Each standard had one or more performance indicators or benchmarks. The indicators were written on a performance grid which indicated what behavior was 'emerging', 'developing', 'proficient', or 'advanced'. Students didn't move through the grades simply because they had occupied a seat for a certain length of time; they only advanced if they mastered the content. It was a sound theory and the main reason I had been interested in working for the school district.

In practice, though, the truth was quite different. Past teachers had been less than rigorous in evaluating the students' work. For example, some of the students told me that previous teachers would give them a printout of the description of the benchmark. The student would google the information and write a paper. The papers I could find that had been saved as artifacts of mastery were horribly written and had no citations. The students had done nothing more than repeat back basic information; I doubted they had truly learned anything in the process.

I knew a standards-based system could work, but I wasn't sure how to transition the kids into a program with more rigorous expectations. They didn't value any work except that which led to mastering a benchmark. They didn't recognize the value in all the assignments that developed the skills leading to mastery.

Yakov E. Netsvetov School

Another problem was that the school looked like a hoarder's home. Everything needed to be cleaned out: file cabinets, book room, offices, and classrooms. Sonja and I were willing to do the work, but we didn't have the authority to discard materials and equipment that the District owned, and no one would give us permission to do so. Additionally, our library needed to convert to an electronic circulation system. I thought we might also need more shelving for the books that were piled up all over the place, though I wasn't sure where the shelves themselves would go. I suggested that we convert to the Library of Congress system at the same time, and offered to do that while spending the summer on the island.

The kids were pretty great. Maybe the worst thing about them was that they were too independent. They were so used to doing everything for themselves or teaching the new teachers every year that they had a hard time remembering that they were the students, not the teachers. Sonja and I both had to work hard to keep the students out of storage areas.

Although no day was ever "typical," the following description represents the average of all the atypical days for a teacher in a two-room schoolhouse:

The alarm went off at 6:30. I hit snooze a couple of times, then walked to the bathroom at 7:00. It was still quite dark at that hour for most of the school year. When I left the bathroom, I went to my office, which was the room where my clothes were hanging. I collected what I needed for the day, went back to my bedroom to get dressed and, of course, play with the dogs. Cody still loved the morning cuddle and play time.

Around 7:30, I let the dogs out, leaving the 3 doors between the outside and the kitchen open so they could come back in. I prepared my breakfast and theirs. My usual breakfast was homemade yogurt with fruit and granola. The fruit was dried or frozen, since fresh fruit was hard to come by. I made iced mocha by the pot, so all I had to do was pour it into a cup.

I had never made yogurt before moving to Atka, but it was hard to buy on the island. I found directions for making it, but I didn't have a food thermometer to know accurately when the mixture reached the correct temperatures. I remembered that Mom's mother, Yiayia, had made her own yogurt. Yiayia wouldn't have used a thermometer to make yogurt any more than the Southern cooks I had taken Home Economics from in high school would have used measuring cups to make biscuits. I channeled my inner Yiayia and figured out other ways to know when the mixture had heated to 200°F and when it had cooled to 110°F.

I left by around 7:55 for my morning commute. The school was about 75 paces from my door. I don't know how long my pace is, but I'm sure this added up to a short commute. If I was the first to arrive—and if my key cooperated—I unlocked the door. There were often several students already waiting, using the school's wifi as they hung around outside. I trained my kids that they could arrive at school any time after the doors were unlocked, but they couldn't enter the classroom until 8:20.

My classroom

When my kids finally entered the classroom, they started working on their journal question. They had 10 minutes from when school started at 8:30 to write at least three complete sentences. Next, we did Daily Oral Language, a proofreading task. In the past, each student had had a book with their personal DOL. It was all individualized by grade level, and the teacher checked the work later. However, I had found with other classes that the students didn't learn anything by doing the exercise unless I talked about the corrections with them. After the ten minutes were up, we started Language Arts.

I learned quickly that the students had minimal writing skills. I was teaching them what should have been a grammar review at the 6th grade level. I also had to teach them the basic formats for writing a paragraph and a five-paragraph essay. Still, they had already shown good improvement in just a short time. I thought they probably had some of the basic skills, but didn't know how to apply them.

The District didn't have a reading program for the

secondary class, so I was using novels. We all did the first book together: *The Bridge to Terabithia*. Once I got a sense of each student's level, I could group them for future novels. I could even create literature units for individuals, if there wasn't anyone else at the same level.

The last 15 minutes of Language Arts was when I read aloud to the students. They enjoyed the first novel I read them, *Stargirl*, by Jerry Spinelli. One of the best parts of reading aloud was that I could read books that were more difficult than the students could read on their own. When I finished *Stargirl*, I read *Ender's Game* by Orson Scott Card.

10:00 to 10:15 was break time. The district bought snacks for the kids, and the procedure for handing out the snacks seemed to have existed for a long time. The snack helper—having an assigned helper to do the work was my contribution—put an assortment of snacks in the bowl. The oldest student picked first, and then the next oldest, on down the line to the youngest.

After the break, it was time for Math. My students ranged from 4th grade math to Geometry. The District used a program that had been designed for homeschoolers. They watched video lessons independently, then worked from a textbook. They learned that I was going to make them go back and correct everything they missed rather than simply mark their answers right or wrong, so it was better to come to me for checking after every lesson segment instead of waiting until the end of a chapter. The big surprise for me was how much I understood in the Algebra I and Geometry curricula. I didn't think I had retained that much, and I know I didn't understand all of it when I took the classes in high school. I had warned the kids at the outset that I might not be able to help much in the higher levels, but it turned out I was wrong about that, much to my relief.

At 11:30, we moved into one of the other classrooms for

Fine Arts. I taught Music for most of the first semester. I had gotten over my shock at how few songs the kids knew, and started to work at giving them a decent foundation in music, including reading musical notation. My jaw dropped when I asked them to sing *Row, Row, Row Your Boat,* and they didn't know it. However, I forged ahead and taught it as we sang. Over several lessons, I introduced the concept of a round. After we sang it in parts a couple of times, I put on a section of *Fantasia*, with Bach's *Toccata and Fugue in Dm*. I told them to pay attention to how the music seemed to echo itself, as if it was playing follow the leader. I compared that with the round, which we sang again.

Lunch time was noon to 1, and there was no school lunch program here. The best part was being able to go home and let the dogs out. Cody and Shadow were always so happy to see me.

The afternoons seemed to fly by. The first 50 minutes was Earth Science. We mostly worked from the text, as we did in Geography, which was the next 50 minutes. I had the freedom to combine or rearrange the two classes, since the information overlapped to some extent. We had another break at 2:45, then at 3:00, my kids went to the gym for P.E. with Sonja, while her kids went to the Art room for Music with me. School dismissed at 3:30.

I stayed at school working on grading and lesson plans until 5:00 most days, then I took the long walk home to greet my dogs and let them out. Sometime in the late afternoon or evening I cooked a meal for myself. No pizza delivery here! I spent the evening watching TV, surfing the internet, and doing chores. Eventually, somewhere around 9:00, I let the dogs out for the last time and got ready for bed.

It would probably have been a boring life for someone else, but I was happy.

One of the things I loved was getting to know the local culture. The Unangax̂ people were subsistence hunters and fishermen, following the traditions of generations of their ancestors. They also gathered foods such as wild celery, berries, and wild rice from the abundance of the tundra. The reindeer herd on the island was the primary source of meat, though sea lions and seals were also hunted. My male students described how they had to carve their own gaff and use it to land a halibut before they were considered adult members of the tribe. Considering that Alaskan halibut often weighed more than 100 pounds, catching one and getting it onto the boat was an exercise in skill and strength.

One of my personal goals was to help my students see the richness of their own culture, which had often been denigrated by "authorities." The parents and grandparents of my students had grown up thinking of their culture as inferior because the "authorities" had told them it was. Generations of children had been kidnapped by the "authorities" to be raised in residential schools. The primary purpose of these schools was to teach them American culture and eradicate any vestige of the Indigenous culture. I wanted my students to understand that cultures can't be compared as superior or inferior, only as different. One chapter of our Geography text listed nine facets of human culture. I assigned the students the task of describing their home in terms of those nine facets. Here are some of their responses.

Family and Social Structure

"There are extended families because everyone's related to everyone basically."

"Almost everyone is related in some way."

"Most of the people that live here stay here."

Agriculture and Industry

"No one on the island farms; all we do is hunt or fish."

"We don't have farms, but we have wild reindeer, birds, and fish. We go hunting or fishing."

"The residents don't really grow plants. If they do grow plants, they keep them indoors."

"One of the main jobs on the island is halibut fishing."

Population

"The population is small, about 60 locals. When the fishing season starts, the population rises by a third."

"In 1990, there were about 80 people living here. Then in 2010 there were around 70, and now there are around 65 people."

"The temporary population is like 65 to 70. The permanent population is like 60-65."

"Some people stay permanently. Some people leave with money."

Rural and Urban Life

"This is a rural area, a big island, and a small village."

Housing

"We live in more modern housing with mainly metal and wood."

"The houses are like a trailer with metal pieces on the outside of the houses."

"The houses come in two pieces, and there are no fences."

"The houses here are made out of wood. It's a three- or four-bedroom house, and some people have warehouses right beside their houses, too."

The Arts

"The arts are basket weaving, native dancing, and kayak making. However, nobody does those arts now."

"Dancing shows how the Aleut people lived and how they survived."

"We have dancers sent to Anchorage to perform."

"If you go to the school in the hallway, they have things in glass cabinets that the students in high school made."

Language

"The common language is English, but most of the local people over 40 speak their Native language."

"All of the people speak English, and the elders that are like 65 years old, they speak Aleut."

"The Aleuts have their own language. It's somewhat Russian."

"The language is fading away, and only the adults speak Aleut."

Religion

"Most residents are Russian Orthodox."

"The people that live in or are from here are Christians."

Customs and Traditions

"Our traditions are fur clothing, wooden hats, and spears for hunting, but those traditions haven't been used for a long time."

"They have Russian Christmas and hunt reindeer."

"The Aleut people used to trade beads to get things from other cultures."

"We believe that the sea otters are our ancestors when they are dead. We never hunt the sea otters unless we have to. Then we use all of the sea otter parts."

Many of my students had last names that attested to the influence of Russia on Alaska. The first outsiders to have contact with the Indigenous populations of Alaska were Russian traders. As Russians settled in Alaska, they intermarried with the Alaskan Natives, as well as starting mission schools. As a result, the predominant religion in parts of Alaska, including the Aleutians, is the Russian Orthodox church. The church building and its cemetery were located in the old part of the village. I was somewhat familiar with Eastern Orthodoxy in general, since my stepfamily was Greek; most were members of the Greek Orthodox church, another national expression of the Eastern Orthodox faith.

The Russian Orthodox celebrate Christmas on January 7-9 because by the time Russia had adopted the Gregorian calendar, there was a difference of 13 days between that and the old Julian calendar. In contrast, when the U.S. adopted the Gregorian calendar at an earlier time, there was a difference of only 11 days. As with other Orthodox denominations, observation of the Feast of the Epiphany was more important among the Russian Orthodox than Christmas Day celebrations.

The Star carried during the Slaavix

The Russian Orthodox church in Alaska had a unique custom called the *Slaavix* or *Starring*. On each of the three nights of the festival, the people walked through the village holding a big decorated star. They went to each house where they had been invited and sang carols. Some were in English, some in Church Slavonic, and I think one or two may have been in Unangam, the language of the Western Aleuts or Unangax. One of the older altar boys held and spun the star during the singing. The last song offered a beautiful blessing to the people in the home: "May God grant you many years!"

After the singing, the host offered the singers some light refreshment. People stayed and talked (and warmed up) for a half hour to an hour before going to the next house. On the final night of the Slaavix, the procession ended at the church.

I joined the Slaavix on the first night. There were song books with the words, but no music notation. I wasn't able to join in singing the transliterated Slavonic and Unangan songs because I found it too hard to try to catch the melody and decipher the words at the same time. However, I caught on to the ones in English after singing them a couple of times.

While we were visiting at one home, Nate, one of my students, handed me a fluffy brown puppy. While I was cuddling her, I commented that I was looking for a little girl puppy. I knew Cody's time as a working dog was ending, and I was thinking ahead to finding and training another service dog. The hostess heard my comment and said, "Take her! She's yours!"

I was surprised and asked if she was sure. She responded, "Merry Christmas!"

Oleana, Nate's mom, was standing near me. She said Nate had wanted her to get a dog and name it Kartuufilax, the Native/Russian word for potato. The pup did bear a striking resemblance to a fluffy potato, so that's what I named her, but I called her Tufa for short.

Cody and Baby Kartuufilax/Scamp get acquainted

I hadn't had a puppy since Beowolf, 18 years earlier. I had to relearn how much work puppies were, but also how sweet and cute they were. Tufa had to learn everything, from eating dry dog food out of a bowl to walking up and down steps. She figured out a way to climb onto the sofa without help. She quickly learned that she was supposed to "potty" when she went outside, but it took longer for her to learn that she was only supposed to potty outside. She was a year old before she could fully grasp that concept, since it was also a matter of getting control of her little body.

Once I understood what the Starring custom was about, I added my name to those who were being visited on the second night. I made a big pot of beef vegetable soup, a cheese spread, and a loaf of sourdough bread. I felt immense happiness when 20-30 people came into my house and started singing; the people carried so much warmth and love with them along with the Star. The custom was a lot like going caroling, except done inside because we were in Alaska, and with a much stronger religious orientation than most caroling I had done in the past.

The dogs behaved well for having that many people in their home. Tufa hid first in her crate and then behind the tree. Shadow greeted everyone, mostly to let them know that he was there to help if they had any food they didn't want to eat. Cody left his hiding place on the bed in my office and worked his way through the room until he was near me, guarding me from all the strangers. I used to have to protect Cody from all the scary things in the world; now he was protecting me.

Cody playing with adolescent Kartuufilax/Scamp

By the time Tufa was four months old, she had lost all the dark fur that made her look like a potato. Her name no longer made sense. I renamed her Scamp because it described her personality perfectly. We were working pretty hard on the house-training thing. It had been an expensive proposition to keep her contained so she couldn't pee all over the house. She had a crate in the bedroom, but I also had to get her a play pen for the living room. It didn't take her long to learn how to climb out of it, so I had to buy a cover for the pen; she learned how to take it off.

Scamp didn't make messes in her personal spaces, but I had to be sure to get her outside regularly. It was a little hard when the weather was bad, until Scamp found a spot under my front porch that wasn't walled in. When the weather was bad, which was most days, Scamp had an outside potty with a roof. She was a smart little thing.

She also had sharp, pointed teeth which she used far too often. She was learning that it was not nice to bite Momma. There was also a limit on what things she was allowed to chew. Any of the dozen or so toys lying on the floor were allowed; my slippers were not, especially when I was in them. Of course, she still chose the slippers—every time.

By the age of four months, Scamp was bigger than Shadow. Her fur was reddish blonde, and she now looked like a small golden retriever with a gorgeous plume of a tail that curved over her back; in later years, I would refer to her as an Alaskan Mala-mutt. She looked just like Jay's dog Buddy, her father. She knew her name, and the word "no"—the things she heard most often. Unfortunately, what I heard most often was the *yap, yap, yap* of a puppy who thought she might get her way if she barked long enough.

The pack dynamic seemed to be that Cody was the leader, and Shadow and Scamp were equal siblings. Cody and Scamp played a game that was mostly about grabbing each other's jaws. Shadow loved to get Scamp to chase him, then he hid so she ran past him. He would show himself to get her attention, and entice her to chase him again.

There had been a few nights when Scamp had let me sleep all night before waking me to go outside. She wasn't a particu-larly cuddly puppy, but she was sweet and affectionate. I guessed as she got older, she would be easier to live with and to handle. At least, that was my hope.

Spring came late to the tundra; March 21 was just another day on the calendar. Spring—which is to say, a bit less winter—started in May. The first sign of the approaching spring was that the snow disappeared from the ground and wasn't replenished. There might be a sprinkling of snow in early spring, but it didn't stay. The mountains remained white, but the whiteness began to retreat until only the tops of the mountains were covered in snow. The air temperatures warmed a bit, but not much, and the air felt heavier because it carried more moisture.

One of the first things I noticed about the spring was bird-song. The eagles and ravens were around all winter, but the small birds that chirped and chattered were absent. Then, one morning, I heard them. I had never noticed their absence, but I was happy to welcome them back.

Bit by bit, dried brown grasses gave way to new green shoots. The greenery spread along the ground, and up the mountains. Just as the snow creeping down the mountains heralded the onset of winter, the green creeping back up showed that spring had arrived.

Seemingly overnight, the tundra burst into bloom. My favorite color is purple, so it made me quite happy that the predominant flower color was purple. There were also some yellow flowers and some white ones, but the only ones I could identify without a guide were dandelions.

As spring continued, the temperature crept up a bit; most days had highs in the 60s. People continued to wear boots, since the ground was marshy. They wore jackets, but not heavy coats. The scarves, ear muffs, and gloves were put away for another winter. There seemed to be more activity locally once school was out because the workers were back at the local seafood processing plant.

There was also a team of scientists on the island, working on identifying contaminated sites left behind by the military after WWII. The residents of Atka had been forced to leave the island during the war, with devastating consequences for the people. Many of the Elders of the village became ill and died while in the detention camp. Losing so many Elders resulted in the loss of the cultural knowledge that those Elders had retained, with no other way for the knowledge to be passed on to younger generations.

Meanwhile, the military had established bases on Atka and its neighbor Adak. When the military had abandoned the base on Atka, they had left behind planes and other equipment, as well as fuel. Over the decades since WWII had ended, the fuel had leached into the soil, contaminating it. The government finally decided to clean up the mess they had made, with a multi-year project to find and decontaminate or remove the affected dirt. The scientists were headquartered at the school and lived in the two school district homes that were empty. I had to put up with a lot of side eyes from the team because they'd been told I was staying in my house rent-free, which wasn't true. I had been offered the opportunity to remain rent-free after school dismissed for the summer, but I had paid rent throughout the school year, as had Sonja, and I thought it was only fair that I continue paying rent until I the day I left in mid-July.

The community dealt with tragedy that summer. The local seafood processing plant, known as "the cannery"—though it

didn't produce anything in cans—was open for the fishing season. There were line workers in the plant itself, as well as workers going out to fish. There were dynamics at play that I didn't totally understand, but apparently the village was not willing to allow the cannery to build housing that was suitable for people to move to

The Cannery, right, as seen looking down the hill from the Clinic

Atka with their families and settle down. The cannery, therefore, was staffed with men, mostly young, who worked for the season (May to November) and then left with a pocketful of cash. Young men who had nothing to entertain themselves with in their off hours was a recipe for trouble.

On a June afternoon, when they finished their shift at the cannery, ten men climbed into a van. I don't know where they were going or why they were in a hurry on that gravel road, but the speed estimates I heard ranged from 60 to 80 miles per hour. As they passed the post office, the driver's leg buckled, causing him to push down on the gas pedal. The van accelerated, hit the edge at the side of the road, and flipped four times. Everyone who wasn't wearing a seat belt was ejected from the van through the windows.

One man died instantly. Another died soon after. A third man also died, but I don't know exactly when it happened. Three people were evacuated to Anchorage. The remaining four, the ones who were wearing seat belts, would end up airlifted to an ER in Anchorage for shoulder and back injuries.

The med-evac plane for the men who were severely injured arrived about four hours after the crash. They sent one plane for all three. Presumably, it took another four hours to get to the hospital in Anchorage. I don't know if the death of the third man would have happened if help had been closer. I found it hard to fathom waiting eight hours to get to a hospital. The island did have a well-equipped ambulance and clinic, and various people trained in emergency first aid, as well as the community health nurse who staffed the clinic, but even an M.D. wouldn't have been of much use without the arsenal of equipment that a small hospital had.

I spent my time after the school year ended on the periphery of Atka, not quite part of the community and yet affected by it. I was an observer, but not an impartial one. I cared about the people there, especially my students. I was shocked and saddened by this horrific accident. I had no doubt that the community was shaken to its core. Injury may have been a constant threat in Atka, mostly among the hunters and fishermen, but death was thankfully rare. When young, healthy people died so tragically and unnecessarily, I couldn't help but pause and wonder why. I prayed in my own way for those who were killed and injured in the crash, for their families, and for the community that had to live with the memory of this traumatic event—and the fear it generated—for the rest of their lives.

Cody seemed to love the spring. Every time we went outside, he rolled in the grass, sticking his legs up in the air and wriggling with a silly grin on his face. He loved his life. He was quite sad after Sonja left for the summer. Her dog Sam, Cody's best friend, was spending the summer up in the village proper, and rarely came down to visit. Cody walked over to their old house and searched for Sam, whimpering as he did so. I tried to tell him that Sam was gone, but Cody could smell that Sam was still around, just not "here." However, Cody was a busy dog with things to do. He shook off his sadness and started his rounds of exploration. As long as he didn't go into the village, he was free to go wherever he liked; the village itself had a leash law. I'm not sure if Cody knew that, but he never went into the village.

Shadow also had a lot of freedom. The fact that he was roughly 1/8 Cody's size didn't seem to inhibit him in any way. The only danger he faced still came from the eagles. One afternoon, the friend who was caring for Sam showed up at my door with Shadow under his arm. He'd found the little guy a half mile down the road, toward the village. He wouldn't have noticed Shadow except that there were eagles circling him overhead. He had grabbed Shadow and brought him home to me before the eagles could snatch him. It was early in the season yet; the salmon weren't running, and the eagles were hungry. For a few days after that, I walked Shadow on his leash. When I let him wander free again, I kept him in sight. As long as he returned when I called him, I could let him be free. If he didn't respond to my voice commands, I put him back on the leash for a walk or two. It was amazing how obedient Shadow became when he again had freedom, but I hoped the salmon would hurry up and get to our island.

By the end of the school year, Scamp was an adolescent pup. She hadn't been well-socialized to humans, mostly because there were so few humans or opportunities for socialization, apart from the group of scientists who were working at the school and living in the District-owned houses around us. Scamp started barking at the strangers and their numerous vehicles, followed by chasing the vehicles. I had to walk her on a leash just to keep her safe. I kept her on a leash in the house, too, because she wasn't responding to my commands anymore when we were outside.

Scamp as an adult

Keeping Scamp on her leash all the time turned out to be exactly what she needed. My reasoning was that being under my control at all times would teach her that all good things came from me; all bad things came from me, too. Her life was better when she behaved in a way that pleased me, so she would learn to behave the way I wanted her to. After a week or two, when we went outside together, Scamp willingly approached the scientists, tail wagging. She ignored their vehicles, except to get out of the way if they were moving toward her.

Inside, Scamp started to initiate play with me. We played Tug and Fetch. When I first tried to teach her Fetch, she wasn't interested, but eventually she started to bring me Ellie, her hot pink stuffed elephant, for me to throw. Repeatedly. It was worse when she wanted me to play with her ball; I called that game Slobber Ball. Why, oh why, had I thought it necessary to teach a retriever how to retrieve?

With the free time I had when school was out, I took all the dogs out for more walks, covering a wider range than before. With Scamp on her leash, we would set off single file through the tall tundra grasses, with Cody in the lead, since he knew where he wanted to go. If I went off in a different direction, Cody turned around and followed us, eventually ending up in front again since Scamp wanted to sniff everything and thus slowed us down. Shadow trotted along behind, keeping me in sight. It was an odd canine version of Follow the Leader.

I had been uncertain about whether or not I was going to keep Scamp when we left the island, and I briefly considered leaving her with Jay. His dog, Buddy, Scamp's father, had died at the end of June after suffering for about three weeks with a bowel obstruction. Buddy was fond of chewing on rocks and bones; it was likely that he had swallowed something which had gotten lodged in his digestive tract. I could see him straining to poop, with little to nothing to show for his efforts. Over time, his back end was covered in dried diarrhea, which was all that he could get out. I tried to help Buddy, dosing him with olive oil, but it didn't help. Getting Buddy to veterinary care was expensive and time-consuming. If Buddy couldn't resolve the problem on his own, he would die, which eventually was what happened. Scamp and Jay were friends, and he would have given her a loving home, but I realized that getting off the island was the only way a dog could be assured of having a long life.

Our relocation to our next home in Craig, Alaska, was logistically rather difficult. The biggest problem would be getting Scamp in her crate, Cody in his service dog harness, Shadow in his carry-on shoulder bag, a suitcase, a backpack, and me all onto the plane from Anchorage to Oregon and then from the plane to the car dealership where I had made arrangements to buy a used car. The trip from Oregon to Craig wouldn't be as bad because we would be taking the new-to-me car onto the ferry. I considered putting Scamp up for adoption in Anchorage, after I got her to a vet for shots and spaying, but ultimately, I decided that Scamp was coming with us no matter what. Dogs aren't disposable; the decision to adopt a dog is a lifelong commitment unless something truly monumental happens. Moving isn't that monumental, no matter how difficult the logistics might be.

We spent a week in Anchorage catching up on routine

healthcare. Unfortunately, Cody's care didn't end up being routine. A blood test showed that there was a problem with his liver. I got the test results the day before we left Anchorage for Oregon, where my brother and his family lived. Fortunately, they lived close to the Oregon State University College of Veterinary Medicine. In the days between my arrival and my nephew's wedding, I was able to get Cody to their Small Animal Clinic for a barrage of testing. Although I would not permit invasive testing, such as a liver biopsy, the vets were able to tell me that Cody most likely had liver cancer. He was 12 years old.

I was shattered to learn that Cody wasn't going to have a long time to enjoy life as a retired service dog. We had worked hard for many years for him to become the happy and independent dog he now was. I had hoped he would have a few 'golden' years of ease as a senior dog. I was disappointed and angry that he and I would be cheated out of that time.

I quickly got on the internet to learn about veterinary care in Craig. There was a vet based in Ketchikan who visited Craig once every month or so. Our ferry to Alaska would dock in Ketchikan, where we would catch another ferry to Prince of Wales Island about four hours later. I made an appointment for Cody to see the vet during our brief stopover.

Cody had no symptoms from the cancer, so it was hard for any of the vets to guess how much longer he had. I got a list of possible problems to watch out for and recommendations of nutritional supplements to support Cody's liver function, while the vet did some blood tests to get baseline data on Cody's condition, which they could use to monitor the progress of the disease. My job was to keep Cody as happy and comfortable as possible in whatever time he had left. We continued on toward our new home.

A relatively minor medical problem in March, 2016, had resulted in my being evacuated by plane from Atka to Anchorage. I realized that I couldn't stay there if adequate healthcare was 1,200 miles and four hours away. I found a teaching position that sounded like a good match in Craig, on Prince of Wales Island. While the island was isolated, it was nowhere near as remote as our previous home; Ketchikan was across the strait, accessible by a three-hour ferry ride or a 30-minute plane trip. While our previous home had had three flights per week for all mail, packages, and passengers, any one of which was usually canceled in an average week, Prince of Wales Island had three flights per day from just one of the aviation companies.

I lived in a 40-year-old, $15,000 trailer, but I had a million dollar view!

Prior to moving to Craig, I had tried to find a place to rent. There were some decent rental properties in Craig, but they were all fairly expensive, and no one was willing to accept a tenant with three dogs. When I saw an old trailer for sale for $15k, I thought it was probably a wise move to buy it. The cost came out about the same as renting an apartment for a year, even with the lot rental; it would almost be like having no rent or house payment in subsequent years if I stayed.

My principal very graciously checked the trailer out for me, mostly to make sure there weren't huge problems with it. However, it was still a 40+ year old single wide trailer, and it showed. There weren't any doors on the closets. The carpet was truly ugly, a sort of brown tweed indoor/outdoor thing. The sofa that was left behind for me was in good shape and comfortable, but much of the vinyl had peeled off; flakes of the red vinyl were all over the house. Some things had been well taken care of.

Within the past two to three years, a new furnace had been installed, a new roof had been put on, the space beneath the trailer had been insulated, and a new kitchen with stainless steel appliances had been installed.

I did a lot of fixing up as soon as I moved in, like getting closet organizers installed in each of the bedroom closets, putting up closet doors, removing built-in shelves, getting them painted, and having them reinstalled where I needed them most. I got the kitchen painted during the first week I was there, from a brown/gold color to a pale pink, which brightened up the room immensely. I also had a fence built in the back yard, along with some remodeling of the existing deck. My next task was to get the sofa reupholstered in a durable purple fabric which could tolerate doggy climbing.

After Atka, Craig seemed huge, with about 1200 residents. It was the largest town on Prince of Wales Island, though there were several other communities. The island's total population was around 5,000. Craig had a grocery store, drug store, assorted businesses, and a handful of restaurants. There were two pizza places, and delivery was sometimes available. Mail wasn't delivered to homes, so everyone had a post office box. If you wanted to run into friends and colleagues, the post office around 4:00 in the afternoon was the place to be.

The school district served Craig only. There were about 250 students split among the elementary, middle, and high schools, as well as an online school; the high school had around 80 students. The entire District had about 70 employees, from the superintendent to the bus drivers, 35 of whom were certified teachers. A dozen teachers worked at the high school either full or part time. I would be teaching special education at the high school.

For such a small school, we offered a varied program for the students. The full-time teachers all wore two hats. For example, one teacher taught English and art, while another taught social studies and Spanish, and a third taught history, language arts, and drama. I wouldn't have anything other than my study skills classes for at least the first semester, but I looked forward to teaching a Home Economics elective after I settled in.

Cody, Shadow, and Scamp seemed happy in Craig. They didn't have the freedom they had had before, but I made the fenced area as large as I could to give them room to play. When I was at home, my to-do list consisted of "let the dog out" and "let the dog in." Each dog operated on their own schedule; the only time they went out together was when there was something outside worth barking at, especially the local black-tailed deer.

I started to find poop near the sliding glass door to the backyard. From the size, it was obviously Cody's. I knew that Cody would never soil inside the house if he had a choice. His cancer was starting to affect him—loss of bowel control was one of the symptoms I had been warned to watch out for.

One December evening, after a particularly difficult day at work, I arrived home wanting to do nothing but vegetate on the sofa. As soon as I walked in, I could smell that Cody had had another accident. When I turned on the lights, though, I started crying; Cody had apparently had diarrhea. More than once. There were piles and puddles of poop all over the kitchen, as well as by the back door. Although I was tired and aching from work, I had no choice but to clean up the mess right then. I was overwhelmed with loneliness, something I struggled with only rarely. It wasn't so much that I wanted someone else to do the cleaning for me (though I wouldn't have said no to an offer of help!), but that there was no one else to see the mess, to commiserate with me, or to help me feel better once I was done. I had grown into an independent person over the years since my divorce, but sometimes I thought independence was overrated.

I put the dogs out, then cried the whole time I was cleaning.

My tears were for me, having this unexpected and nasty task to do, and for Cody, who was at last showing symptoms of his liver cancer. He probably expected to be punished for the mess; *I* knew I would never scold him for something he couldn't control, but *he* didn't. I was frankly grateful he had made his messes on the vinyl kitchen floor and not the carpet. When I was finished cleaning, I let the dogs back in. I gave Cody some extra hugs and kind words, just in case he was apprehensive.

I decided to buy a doggy door for the sliding glass doors to the deck. Most of Cody's messes had been by that door. I thought if he could get outside independently, perhaps he would be able to avoid making messes inside. The panel was fairly easy to install. Scamp learned how to go in and out right away, and I used her as a model for Cody. Shadow never learned to use the door; the opening was 8" off the ground. Shadow pretended not to be able to reach it, though he was miraculously able to come back in if he was outside at mealtime. Cody eventually learned how to use the door, but it took a lot of treats and encouragement; he didn't like feeling the plastic flap on his head or back. However, he never had another accident in the house.

The only other noteworthy event during this time was that I started reading about Autism Spectrum Disorders (ASD). My colleagues and I thought one of our students should be evaluated for possible ASD. I was hoping to find more specific information on how teens on the mild end of the Spectrum behaved in order to support the evaluation request. As I read, I was startled to realize I had many characteristics of mild ASD, or what used to be called Asperger's Syndrome. I had actually said to others many of the things the books I consulted listed as thoughts or beliefs of "Aspies." As a special ed teacher, I had always loved working with that particular type of child; I saw meeting their learning needs as puzzles to be solved. How did they see the world? How did they learn? How could I help?

Suddenly, I realized I presented the same puzzle to others.

I also realized autism might be the key to understanding why I had never performed well in the workplace. My supervisors and colleagues over the past 30 years had tried to figure out why someone as intelligent and well-educated as I was didn't know how to speak or act appropriately in the workplace. They considered it a shame someone who was so skilled and knowledgeable inside the classroom was so difficult to get along with outside the classroom. They were trying to solve my puzzle, but they had no frame of reference. If they had observed my behavior through the lens of autism, would they have been able to help me become a better employee? Was it still possible I could learn the skills I needed?

I was not invited to return to Craig High School for a second year because of these same problems. I felt angry because the first time I heard I wasn't meeting expectations was three-fourths of the way though the school year, and there was no documentation to support that decision. Alaska law allowed a school district not to retain non-tenured teachers for any reason or no reason at all; I had no recourse and no job. My only comfort was in recognizing that my ASD, if in fact it existed, was the true cause of my professional problems.

I loved Craig. The people were warm and welcoming. My little trailer was turning into a comfortable home. My dogs were happy. The setting was gorgeous; the natural beauty all around me fed my soul. No one minded if I behaved like a hermit. I didn't have the money to move, but I didn't want to anyway. I decided to remain in Craig and search for work I could do online.

Cody's Final Chapter Warning

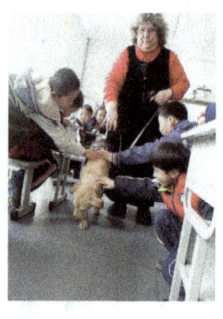

Cody visits my classroom in China

A NOTE FROM LAUREN:

I had to write this chapter. You don't have to read it, though I hope you will. You can safely skip to the Epilogue. If you choose to read it, have a handkerchief nearby.

Chapter 15

Cody's Final Chapter

I went to NC to visit my mother early in July, 2017. I was away for about a week. I left the dogs at home with McKenna, a pet sitter they knew and loved. When I returned home, Cody seemed a little subdued, though happy to see me. Within a couple of days, though, I noticed his behavior had changed. He hadn't eaten much while I was gone,

Cody enjoys Spring on the tundra

which was normal, but his appetite hadn't rebounded once I was home. His ribs were starting to show. I was afraid the cancer was winning the battle Cody and I had been waging against it.

I made an appointment for Cody to see the same vet who had seen him in Ketchikan the previous year and intermittently on Prince of Wales Island since then. Although Cody had officially retired from service the year before, I put his harness on him for the ferry ride over to Ketchikan; otherwise, he would have had to ride in my car below deck. I was afraid the vet would tell me there was nothing more we could do for him. I steeled myself for the possibility of making the return trip to Craig without Cody.

The visit to the vet went well, or at least better than expected. I was relieved when she told me explicitly it wasn't time to put Cody down. She didn't have to add the word "yet." She told me to keep giving him the liver supporting supplements he'd been on for the past year. She also gave me gabapentin to use as a painkiller. I gave Cody a pill for the three-hour ferry ride home. He fell asleep on a bench seat. In fact, he was so soundly asleep that I couldn't wake him when one of the ferry employees demanded that Cody move to the floor. I apologized for having let him up on a bench seat, since that had been my fault. I told her he was dying of cancer and in a drugged sleep. He had already "contaminated" the seat. He would wake up if we tried to move him. Couldn't we let the dog stay in place? She was adamant that we follow the rules, though she couldn't produce any written rules when I asked. Nonetheless, I woke Cody to have him sleep on the floor where dogs belonged. When we docked, I had to lift him to his feet and support his weight with his harness while he shuffled his way to the car. I thought at least Cody wouldn't be in pain if the pills knocked him out every time he took them.

As it turned out, the ferry trip was the only time those pills had a sedative effect on Cody. I suspect he slept so soundly because it was the first time in a long while that he hadn't had pain. Over the next two weeks, I saw he was in more severe pain more often. I contacted the vet again, asking for options, but she didn't return my email. Not hearing from her, I assumed she had no options to offer.

I finally called a different vet, also in Ketchikan, to schedule euthanasia for Cody on Thursday. They had never treated Cody, but they returned my message. They asked me when and where they should pick him up. Many people on our island would send their pets over for euthanasia by ferry or plane. The vets' offices were used to picking up these unaccompanied pets and putting them down. Cody would have been frightened to travel without me. After all we had been through together, I couldn't abandon him right at the end. I would have to put Cody in his harness yet again. I made the ferry reservations for us to travel and secured a spot for my car.

Cody had started sleeping on the floor beside my bed. He tended to do that in warmer weather anyway, but I had the impression climbing up the steps to the platform bed took more energy than he had left. When we went to bed on Wednesday night, the night before Cody was scheduled to be put down, I picked him up and placed him on the bed with me and the other dogs. I wanted us to have one last morning cuddle.

Putting Cody on the bed for his last night was my first mistake.

When I taught young children, I would help them down from playground equipment if they climbed up so high that they got scared, but I never picked kids up and placed them on the equipment. I reasoned the risk of their falling was too great to leave them on a climber if they were afraid. On the other hand, I also figured they weren't safe on the equipment if they couldn't climb up by themselves. I violated my own logic by putting Cody on the bed when he couldn't get up there himself.

In the morning, Cody was on his side on the floor next to the bed. His eyes were closed, and his body was cold. At first, I thought he was dead, until I saw his chest move as he breathed. Cody didn't look like he could survive the trip to Ketchikan; I knew he would not be able to wear his harness and "pass" as a service dog.

My second mistake was forgetting that I could have let Cody ride the ferry in my car below deck.

I spent the next five days taking care of Cody on his

deathbed. He remained cold to the touch. He trembled with every breath. I lay beside him, petting him. I talked softly to him, even though I knew he was mostly deaf. I gave him the gabapentin; if it made him sleep, at least he wouldn't be in pain. I placed a quilt on him and a pillow under his head. Even Scamp helped, letting me know if Cody cried or needed me, lying beside him, and bringing him her favorite toys. There was no vet on the island, and the vet's Ketchikan office wouldn't return my calls. No one was available to help me, and I didn't know how to help Cody. I had never felt so alone and useless in my life.

Cody and I both slept on my L-shaped sofa, our heads meeting at the corner. Cody got decent sleep overnight; a couple of shots of rum were pretty helpful in helping him sleep. I didn't drink; I did, however, make my own vanilla extract. I had previously used vodka, but now I used white rum. I was glad I had it available if it helped Cody.

Friday morning, Cody insisted on getting off the sofa and going outside. I left him on the deck and went into the bedroom to dress. It started to rain. When I came back out of the bedroom, Cody had gotten himself back inside and was lying on the floor in the kitchen. I offered him food, which he refused, but he lapped up the water. I started to wonder if I had misread what had happened Thursday morning. When I found Cody lying on the floor beside the bed, it was possible he had fallen off the bed and gotten hurt rather than being weak from the cancer's progress. He spent the rest of Friday on the floor or the sofa, crying and complaining.

Cody wasn't any better on Saturday, but he stopped crying and seemed more okay with my being out of his sight. His hearing loss, which had been a blessing in dealing with loud noises over the past year, now made it impossible for me to call out reassurances to him. I took him down the deck steps in his work harness, which let me carry most of his weight, leaving him sitting up in the grass. He rolled over on his side to take a nap. He didn't seem to have any obvious pain or discomfort. I decided to let him stay out there until he asked to come back in. As I was cleaning Cody's bedding, it started to rain again. Just as I heard the first drops, Cody called me to come get him. I settled him on his freshly made bed, after which he took a deep, restful nap.

I'm not a nurse; I'm a teacher. While I could be extremely calm and rational during a first aid emergency, I didn't know how to provide ongoing care for Cody. I eventually figured out how to keep him comfortable, but it took some trial and error. I worried Cody's bodily fluids would permanently damage my newly reupholstered sofa. I ended up removing some of the sofa cushions and scrubbing their surfaces in the shower. I laid an old shower curtain liner where the missing cushions belonged, and placed a quilted bedspread on the plastic curtain. I used puppy pads under Cody's bottom to catch anything that might leak; I put another one under his head, on top of the pillow, to catch drool and spilled liquids. I kept Cody covered with the quilt and changed his bedding twice a day, replacing the quilt with another and throwing the soiled quilt in the wash.

From the moment Cody woke up from his Saturday nap and all through Sunday, he cried constantly. When he was awake, he was in pain. Nothing I did seemed to make a difference. I tried everything I could think of. He couldn't lift his head anymore, so he could only drink from a syringe; I filled one with rum over and over. I also had some bacon-flavored CBD oil for dogs; I gave him dropperfuls of that, too. Since I didn't know anything about the strength of the drops, I paired them with blowing cannabis smoke in his nose. I hoped at least one of the three would work. I wasn't worried about killing him with an overdose; I knew his pain and my inability to help would make his death a blessing for both of us. He watched me with eyes filled with love and pain, trusting me to make him feel better. I wished I could.

After Cody had fallen asleep, I went outside and prayed to a God I didn't believe in. I had wanted Cody to have a good death, like Beowolf had had. I had wanted him to relax and drift away with me there petting him and murmuring his name. Now all I wanted was for him to die.

I walked back in and knelt in front of Cody's bed. I rested my head against him, tears running down my face, and apologized for anything I had ever done wrong, but especially for the mistakes I had made that had led to this horrible, painful, lingering death. I told him how much I loved him, how special he was, how he had made a difference in my life, and how he had made a difference in the world. And how sorry I was. And how much I loved him. And how sorry I was. I think I cried more tears at Cody's bedside than I had ever cried before.

By Monday morning, I was frantic to find help. I even asked my own doctor if she could help minimize Cody's pain, but of course she was legally constrained from offering assistance. There wasn't anyone available anywhere who could help me relieve Cody's suffering. I contacted the vet who had been going to perform the euthanasia, but that office was closed on Mondays. The other clinic had to check with their vet to see if she would prescribe a pain medication. I posted on Facebook asking if anyone local had a solution for getting Cody either pain relief or death. One person I didn't even know had some sedative syringes that had been prescribed for a cat during travel and never used. We met at a coffee shop to pass the drugs and laughed about how nefarious that sounded.

I looked up the drug in the syringes to see what kind of dose was appropriate. It turned out Cody could take two of the cat doses at a time. By the time the second dose was due, the

Ketchikan vet's office had called back to say they had called in a prescription for Cody. The person on the phone went out of her way to tell me they were only doing this out of sympathy for Cody. I was furious at that comment. This was the vet's office that had followed Cody since before we ever set foot on Prince of Wales Island. This was the vet's office that had prescribed the pain medication that no longer worked. And this was the vet's office that had just given Cody his most recent blood tests not even three weeks earlier. Their obligation to Cody was as his primary care provider, not as a bystander trying to relieve suffering. I was too angry to respond to her insensitivity; I just thanked them for their help.

Cody had spent the whole day crying with every breath. The only time he stopped was when he could see me; my putting my hand on him wasn't enough to comfort him anymore. He calmed down once the prescribed pill took effect. I had to make some decisions and plans while he was finally quiet.

The vet who had been going to do the euthanasia would open Tuesday, the next day. The ferry left at 7:00, but the vet didn't open until after that. I would have to take Cody over on the Wednesday ferry, at the earliest. I couldn't call the vet until the next morning, but I could go online and make the ferry reservation right away. I knew I would have to have my car to transport Cody, and there was a limit on how many vehicles the ferry could hold. The sooner I made the reservation, the better.

I went to bed and set an alarm to wake me at 1:00 so I could give Cody his pain pill. When I woke up, he was sleeping peacefully. I decided I would let him sleep instead of dosing him. During the previous four nights I had awakened every time Cody had made a noise, or so it had felt. If Cody was in pain, I was sure he'd let me know.

I woke a little after 6:00 Tuesday morning, in time to watch

Cody take his last breaths. His eyes slowly went out of focus. I petted his ears with one hand and put the other on his chest. His heart slowed to a flutter and stopped. Cody died at 6:20 a.m. on August 1, 2017, with my caress on his body and my kiss on his forehead.

I gave him one last command: "Free Dog!"

Epilogue

Cody, in October, 2012

I KEPT the reservation on the ferry for the day after Cody died and transported his body to Ketchikan. The vet who would have done the euthanasia arranged for cremation instead. Keith wanted Cody's ashes; Cody was the last remaining dog we had shared.

I was distraught, not so much for the fact Cody was gone, but because of the way he had died. After being without a therapist for five years, I had to go back into therapy to process what had happened. I learned that even though Cody had suffered in ways neither humans nor pets suffer in our modern medical age, I had done everything possible to relieve his pain. He had known right up to the end that I loved him.

A month or so after Cody died, I adopted a kitten. He had a somewhat distinguished air, so I named him Sir, and waited for his behavior to demonstrate what his "sir-name" should be. Sir and Scamp were fast friends within a week; Shadow and Sir eventually formed their own friendship, though I think mutual tormentors might be a better description.

A few months after Cody's death, I received a formal diagnosis of an Autism Spectrum Disorder. I continue to work on

understanding how it has affected me throughout my life and career and what it means for me going forward. I applied for and was reinstated to Social Security Disability Income, which alleviated the need for me to find work while I was trying to gain the social skills necessary to be successful.

While we lived in China, friends had said I should write a book about Cody. His life even at that point had been filled with

Sir-the-Cat as an adult

adventures most Americans would never have. I liked the idea, but I thought I couldn't write the book until I knew how it ended. I wrote some of the early chapters during the spring and summer of 2017, but once I knew the end of Cody's story, I no longer had the heart to write it. It took a few months—and a few therapy sessions—before I could write about Cody's life without crying; I still cried the whole time I was writing "Cody's Final Chapter."

Why did I write Cody's memoir?

This book is Cody's legacy to the people he didn't meet in life. He inspired those he met with his ability to overcome his past and not just survive, but thrive. Cody's story inspired mine as well. While he was part of my life, I, too, became broken. Cody inspired me in my own healing process to become an independent and self-reliant woman. If Cody, damaged as he was, could turn into the dog he eventually became, I could transform, too.

Cody was as broken as a dog could be, yet he never lost his capacity to accept and give love. Over time, his willingness and openness to be part of a human/dog pack healed him. While he always needed a somewhat therapeutic environment and humans who were responsive to his needs, Cody deserves all the credit for recreating himself. It had taken many years, but Cody, the former Pinocchi-dog, had transformed into a Real Dog. No Blue Fairy had waved her wand over Cody's head; the only magic needed was love.

Acknowledgments

Thank you as always to Lindsey McLeod, the editor and book midwife who challenges me to be the best writer I can.

Thank you to Emilija Rakić, of Emily's World of Design, who created the perfect cover for Cody's memoir. Thanks to you, his images will live forever.

Thank you to the manuscript readers who offered feedback: Coralee Binder, Wanda Frazier, and Sharon Moser. You were an important part of polishing this book and getting it ready for publication.

To the important people who are mentioned, named or not, within the pages of this story: You played a part in Cody's life and mine. I am grateful for your contributions to our growth.

To those who weren't mentioned but were still important, especially friends and family: Thank you for the care and support you offered along the way, both as I lived my life and as I wrote and published this memoir.

A special note of thanks to the Facebook group Pot Smoking Atheists who Love Dogs: Thank you for all the advice and feedback you offered during the publication process. You are my pack!

About the Author

Lauren has filled many roles in her life, including educator, Girl Scout leader, linguist, songwriter, crafter, and, most importantly, mother and grandmother. Since getting her first dog in 1995, Lauren has worked with dozens of dogs as a shelter volunteer and a foster parent. She has lived with a long list of wonderful canine companions, most of whom are mentioned in this book.

Lauren is also the author of **Satan's Therapist**, available on Amazon <https://www.amazon.com/>. Lauren lives in a log cabin in North Pole, Alaska, along with Shadow, a grumpy poodle, Shenanigans, a service-dog-in-training, and Sir-the-Cat, who runs the household.